CREATING
AN ETHICAL POSITION
IN FAMILY THERAPY

Other titles in the

Systemic Thinking and Practice Series

edited by David Campbell & Ros Draper
published and distributed by Karnac Books

Bentovim, A.   *Trauma-Organized Systems. Systemic Understanding of Family Violence: Physical and Sexual Abuse*

Bor, R., & Miller, R.   *Internal Consultation in Health Care Settings*

Campbell, D., Draper, R., & Huffington, C.   *Second Thoughts on the Theory and Practice of the Milan Approach to Family Therapy*

Campbell, D., Draper, R., & Huffington, C.   *Teaching Systemic Thinking*

Cecchin, G., Lane, G., & Ray, W. A.   *The Cybernetics of Prejudices in the Practice of Psychotherapy*

Cecchin, G., Lane, G., & Ray, W. A.   *Irreverence: A Strategy for Therapists' Survival*

Daniel, G., & Burck, C.   *Gender and Family Therapy*

Draper, R., Gower, M., & Huffington, C.   *Teaching Family Therapy*

Fruggeri, L., et al.   *New Systemic Ideas from the Italian Mental Health Movement*

Hoffman, L.   *Exchanging Voices: A Collaborative Approach to Family Therapy*

Inger, I., & Inger, J.   *Co-Constructing Therapeutic Conversations: A Consultation of Restraint*

Jones, E.   *Working with Adult Survivors of Child Sexual Abuse*

Mason, B.   *Handing Over: Developing Consistency across Shifts in Residential and Health Settings*

Ray, W. A., & Keeney, B. P.   *Resource-Focused Therapy*

Smith, G.   *Systemic Approaches to Training in Child Protection*

Work with Organizations

Campbell, D.   *Learning Consultation*

Campbell, D., Coldicott, T., & Kinsella, K.   *Systemic Work with Organizations: A New Model for Managers and Change Agents*

Campbell, D., Draper, R., & Huffington, C.   *A Systemic Approach to Consultation*

Huffington, C., & Brunning, H.   *Internal Consultancy in the Public Sector: Case Studies*

McCaughan, N., & Palmer, B.   *Systems Thinking for Harassed Managers*

Credit Card orders, Tel: 071-584-3303; Fax: 071-823-7743

CREATING
AN ETHICAL POSITION
IN FAMILY THERAPY

Ivan B. Inger
&
Jeri Inger

Systemic Thinking and Practice Series

Series Editors
David Campbell & Ros Draper

London
KARNAC BOOKS

This edition first published in 1994 by
H. Karnac (Books) Ltd.
58 Gloucester Road
London SW7 4QY

British Library Cataloguing in Publication Data

Inger, Ivan B.
    Creating an Ethical Position in Family
    Therapy. — (Systemic Thinking & Practice
    Series)
    I. Title II. Inger, Jeri III. Series
    616.89156

    ISBN: 1–85575–071–6

Printed in Great Britain by BPC Wheatons Ltd, Exeter

To the families we have known, cared for, and loved,
especially our own,
for they have taught us all we know.

CONTENTS

EDITORS' FOREWORD   ix

Chapter one
Roving through the fields of psychotherapy:
an overview   1

Chapter two
Individualism, family, and psychotherapy   5

Chapter three
Family therapy and change   17

Chapter four
Evolving an ethic of being   21

Chapter five
Practising from an ethical perspective   37

Chapter six
A consultation with a therapist, a family,
and an audience   53

Chapter seven
Reflections   113

REFERENCES   117

INDEX   121

EDITORS' FOREWORD

In the increasingly complex world in which we live, there are a greater number of diverse points of view, or discourses, put forward on any issue. For example, minority groups add new voices to the debate about how we should live our social lives, and many people are questioning traditional institutions such as religion and marriage. All of this means that there are fewer and fewer absolutes to guide our lives, and if this is so then we are all left to ourselves to evaluate what is going on and to make decisions about how we live our lives. This is the ethical position.

However, the Ingers take this process one step further by saying that the values that underlie our decisions are created through an interactional process. Although we have to take responsibility for our own ethical position, we only achieve it by creating ideas through social exchange. While this process takes place on a daily basis through a thousand exchanges with other people and with the trappings of our society, it also occurs in the relationship between therapist and client. The ethical position described in this book is that which allows both the therapist and the client to own their presuppositions and understand the effect that they have on their

lives. The authors explore the possibility that taking ethical positions is at the heart of what is "therapeutic" about family therapists'
work.

This book is an important addition to the Series because much
systemic thinking and practice has run the risk of becoming un-
tethered from its value base. For example, the concept of neutrality
has been misconstrued by many therapists, and it is only in the last
few years that many people have reexamined the values and the
ethics of their work.

The book also introduces some new ideas into the therapeutic
dialogue through the work of Martin Buber. Concepts such as the
distinction between "I–Thou" and "I–It" relationships are similar
but different enough from familiar family therapy formulations to
challenge therapists to think differently about their work. As with
the other book the Ingers produced in this series, they allow the
reader to learn by observing them work, in this case by studying
their transcript, and thereby drawing their own conclusions.

David Campbell
Ros Draper
London
October, 1994

CREATING
AN ETHICAL POSITION
IN FAMILY THERAPY

CHAPTER ONE

Roving through the fields of psychotherapy: an overview

Mungojerrie and Rumpelteazer are two cats in T. S. Eliot's *Old Possum's Book of Practical Cats* (1939). They are described as ". . . a very notorious couple of cats . . . knockabout clowns, quick-change comedians, tight-rope walkers and acrobats." As a couple of family therapists we have often felt like entertainers, walking the ever-present tightrope of therapy—always ready for the quick-change from being tightrope walkers to being the net. T. S. Eliot's cats roved through the neighbourhoods of London, and we have roved through the fields of psychotherapy and philosophy, taking this and that from different areas and trying them on for size, effect, and meaning. In fact, we have been incurable rovers in the fields of science, philosophy, literature, and cultural anthropology. One could say that our roving through the world of ideas and meanings as an aesthetic experience has been our work. Yet, as practical cats we have put forth considerable effort applying an aesthetic perspective to the practice of psychotherapy (Inger & Inger, 1990a, 1990b). In order to ensure that aesthetics and practices of psychotherapy form a harmonious complementarity, we have turned to ethics.

1

Ethics is a set of habits and customs about how to relate to one another. Ethics is a way of organizing our conduct and meanings when we are in contact with one another. These habits and customs allow us to maintain continuity in relationships and to have expectations about ourselves and others in different relational contexts. The ethics of our professional practices reflect the attitudes with which we construct relationships among ourselves and with clients. Ethics informs us of the nature of the fit between our beliefs and the beliefs of others, and how we put our beliefs into practice. By taking responsibility for how we think and behave relative to the ideas and behaviours of others, we get some notion of how those ideas and actions impact on clients. Clients' beliefs and practices impact on us as well. Thus, ethics of practice has come to mean how we impact on clients with our views of ourselves and them, and reciprocally how they impact on our beliefs and practices. This mutuality of influence is the foundation stone of an ethical perspective for psychotherapy.

* * *

Mungojerrie and Rumpelteazer are said to have had ". . . a wonderful way of working together. And some of the time you would say it was luck, and some of the time you would say it was weather" (Eliot, 1939). Our work together, like that of Mungojerrie and Rumpleteazer, has been a mixture of luck and weather. As we discuss in chapters two and three, much of our experience in the psychotherapy area has felt like being in a whirlwind, a hurricane, and as unpredictable as the weather. As a team working together, we have had a Mungojerrie- and Rumpelteazer-like existence. We have often wondered which changes in the families have been the product of our individual efforts and which have been the result of our collective experience. It is difficult if not impossible to sort out. Over the past two decades of roving around and trying out different ideas, we have found ourselves in many engulfing and unpredictable situations, but, through all the turbulence, the process of being in dialogue with others (colleagues and clients) has been the most valuable aspect of the work.

In the process of our evolution as psychotherapists, we have moved from being individual psychotherapists to being family therapists. Much of this transition was based on ethical notions,

notions about attachment and the need for connection and confirmation among humans—connection for the sake of the individual and the collective. As our ideas about psychotherapy broadened from individual to family, they increased in scope from metaphors based on physical science to those based on philosophy, arts, and literature, thereby bringing aesthetics directly into psychotherapy.

This evolution has been a freeing experience. As we shed the bonds of "objectivity" and the shackles of the scientific method, we found ourselves looking to ethics as a guide. As the field around us became more enamoured with change, especially quick change, we found it increasingly important to focus on ethics by practising, teaching, and writing from that perspective. It has been helpful to look to other fields for continued guidance about the place of ethics in human interactions. Anthropology, philosophy, and the performing arts are close to the heart of both ethics and family therapy, as they each remain devoted to asking overarching questions about observation, participation, and human interactions. They remind us of the need to have continued respect for the human condition in all of its complex vicissitudes.

In chapter four, we present examples of crises of uncertainty. Three people—the fictional character of Dr. Richard Dysart (from the play *Equus*), Martin Buber, and Tom Andersen—each experience internal dilemmas about different circumstances. They each come through a crisis of uncertainty with a sense of personal ethics that is different from the certainty of "objectivity" that was in place before the crisis. We identify with these people, even though our experience was less than of crisis proportions and more of an evolution. We nonetheless have come along the same route in our rovings through many different experiences as psychotherapists.

Through our interest in philosophy, we came across the ideas of Martin Buber. As a result, we have incorporated many of his concepts into our work over the past several years. These ideas, presented throughout the book, but particularly in chapter five, include "imagining the real and inclusion", "being with ourselves", "bending towards others", and "experiencing the between". These philosophical constructs are given lengthy exposition in the text so that readers can familiarize themselves with these ideas and their attendant practices as they read about how they are constructed and the beliefs that support them.

In chapter six, we present an interview with a family. The interview is part of a workshop that includes an audience of family therapists who participate in hypothesizing and debriefing the experience. The audience, the family, and we as interviewers all struggle with uncertain feelings and changing thoughts throughout the process of the interview. The experience ends in a way that is different from what was anticipated by all. It is our hope that the process of our thinking is clarified through the demonstration of our ideas and the annotation of our thoughts, and that we leave the reader with some reflections on a family therapy interview based on an ethical perspective.

CHAPTER TWO

Individualism, family, and psychotherapy

Roving

Our roving in the fields of science, art, and literature began when we were students in the 1960s. There were so many intriguing ideas and so many things to do. We were caught up in the whirlwind of aesthetic ideas and pragmatic solutions to the problems confronting life in all its facets. It was an exciting time to be a learner. Like many 1960s university students, we had a bent towards the humanities. We had heard about the ideas and ideals of the philosopher Martin Buber. We were especially familiar with his I–Thou relationship (Buber, 1958). We had one or two of his books on our shelves and were pleased to have Buber in our library, but we had not read him. His ideas seemed a bit esoteric and spiritual, and he was difficult to read. That was enough to deter us. It was acceptable just to say we believed in the I–Thou relationship. And using the I–Thou phrase was sufficient for expressing our belief in the need for mutuality in relationships and respect for one another. Everyone seemed to understand. For over two decades Buber sat on the shelf while we immersed ourselves in the applied science of psychotherapy. We immersed ourselves in the thinking and

5

practices of such *mavens* of mind as Freud, Jung, Sullivan, Fromm, Horney, Mahler, Guntrip, Winnicott, Anna Freud, Erik Erickson, and many others. We had bought into the scientific paradigm and believed it would help solve many of life's dilemmas.

Our sojourn as psychotherapists started in the early 1970s and, like many others of that era, we thought we were knowers of the human psyche. We had studied the subject and had clinical training from competent teachers. Our professional beliefs about psychology and psychotherapy were gleaned from standard psychological texts and mainstream psychotherapy literature. Psychotherapy was predominantly for individuals and only tangentially for families. At best, family therapy was an adjunct to individual therapy. Texts were filled with notions about the individual as a self-contained entity, and these texts described and explained what deprived some of us from growing up as so-called normal individuals. They usually described the individual's internal psychological state as a collection of organized negative attributes or deficits which, working deductively, explained what things went wrong during a person's formative years. Families (mostly mothers) were seen as the cause of the development of these negative attributes or deficits that resided within the individual.

As we knocked about in the fields of psychotherapy, we came across many ideas and practices that troubled us and made us uneasy about the way we thought about people and the methods we used in the process of psychotherapy. From time to time, we would hearken back to our earlier exposure to the humanities and wonder if we were on the wrong path. During these times, we would seriously question ourselves about the legitimacy of our efforts. A particularly troublesome point was that the focus of mainstream psychological theory was on processes internal to the individual. Blame for what went wrong was ascribed to family members (mostly mothers), who were themselves usually told to work things out in their own individual psychotherapy. The marriage unit, the nuclear family, the extended family, the community, and the culture were all overlooked or minimized. They were often kept out of the therapy room—it was reserved for the individual. In fact, most psychotherapies honoured the rights of the individual over and against family and community by promoting separation over attachment. Healthy development was believed to require the early separation of the individual from his family of origin. This was especially thought to be true for the male child. Attachment for the male was considered of secondary importance to that of the state of self-reliance and self-containment.

Mothers, fathers, and children

We had been steeped in theories of child development in our wanderings, and we thought we had gained a certain proficiency of knowledge about how children develop and how families participate in that development. Yet, we were continually confronted with a theme that ran throughout these developmental theories: namely, negative ideas about attachment and the positive ideas about progressive separations towards autonomy. For the male child this state of individualism seemed attainable only through acts of "severation", acts that discouraged the continuance of intimate attachment to members of his family of origin. Parents (again, mostly mothers, as fathers were still, for the most part, excused from intimate and consistent participation) were expected to be prepared for the inevitable separation that would take place. The idea of a complete emotional separation was put forth as being in the best interests of the developing male child. The mother was expected to be self-effacing and accepting of the inevitable emotional separation from her son. The emphasis on separation did not take into account the meaning that the separation had on the parents and the impact that that emphasis has had on the entire ecology of family relationships.

Silverstein (Walters, Carter, Papp, & Silverstein, 1988) summarized the dilemma a mother faces after raising a son.

> The mother of sons, then, stands in the position of having to create her complementary opposite, someone destined to behave in a way that works to keep both mothers and sons locked into the established social structure, and perhaps also locked in opposition to each other. A mother does not necessarily act to her personal advantage when she acts as the agent and nurturer of male authority. [p. 160]

Mothers were to turn their sons towards the outer world and away from themselves in a way that had to be painful for both mothers and sons throughout their adulthoods. This form of separation demanded emotional distance and a disavowal of all the successful nurturing that went into his childhood years. There seemed to be a "conspicuous silence", even among women authors, about the impact of separation on the mother and the lifelong consequences that the practice of separation has had on both of them (Silverstein, in Walters et al., 1988).

The situation for mothers and daughters seemed different. Mothers were to maintain their relationships with their daughters, while the daughters separated just enough to be able to produce and nurture the next generation of children. Yet, both mothers and daughters were expected to continue their attachment because they provided the continuity between the generations and between the families. Adult daughters were to raise children and prepare for separations from sons while maintaining attachments with daughters (Walters et al., 1988). The mother/daughter relationship allows for the continuity of attachment among women but leaves men out in the world in their own self-contained, personal bubbles.

Both sons and daughters had to be satisfied with minimal and often discontinuous relational contact with fathers. Separation was not as problematic with and for fathers since intimate attachment had probably not taken place for them in the way it had for mothers and children. But what about these amorphous attachments with fathers? How did they affect the life of the family? And what about the emphasis on the separation of males and the lack of continuity of their attachments? Does the discontinuity of their relationships reflect the essentially different values placed on attachment and separation for males and females? These differences are highly emotionally charged, confusing, and impactful on family members throughout their lifetimes.

The male characteristics of self-reliance and self-containment, through successive separations, represent the dominant societal metaphor for how to be a person in the world. The shorthand for the metaphor is individualism. Individualism is a social construct which celebrates individual achievement as the highest form of personal status in society. This form of individualism is characterized by the drawing of a sharp but imaginary boundary between self and other, with a reliance on the ability to be in control of one's self (Sampson, 1985, 1988). It often means that individuals isolate themselves from the support of family and community, paradoxically creating other forms of dependency. Self-contained individualism emphasizes a self that is exclusionary, thus rendering individuals to imagine themselves alone but in control of their own bodies and minds. When self-contained individualism is contrasted to ensembled individualism (Sampson, 1988, p. 16) we see that the latter is characterized by a more fluid boundary between self and other and a willingness to be part of a matrix of relationships that determines control. Ensembled individuals are a part of a field of persons in which boundaries between self and other are more fluid and permeable. Individuals see themselves as inclusive with others, a part of a circle of self plus others. Sampson (1988) points out that as one becomes inclusive with others, then others can become a part of the definition of self. Self-contained individualists, on the other hand, are entities separate from the circle of others.

After a while, we stopped roving, stopped collecting ideas, and settled comfortably into a practice in the field of individual psychotherapy. It appeared to us that we had reached stasis, a point of self-satisfied equilibrium. We had arrived in our chosen work. We were like the two practical cats, Mungojerrie and Rumpleteazer, who cruised through neighbourhoods "doing their thing". We worked at our trade and did not realize, until we started to work with families, that we had dug ourselves into a hole. Our work was exclusively about individuals, and encapsulated individuals at that. We had been promoting the self-contained individual. When we started working with families we found that we were working with many individuals simultaneously, all of whom demanded attention about their individuality exclusive of each other. It was during the early period of our work with families that we came to realize the extent to which the fields of psychotherapy promoted self-contained individualism over ensembled individualism or the collective interests of the family unit.

Individualism

Self-contained individualism has reigned supreme in the psychotherapy fields. Individual psychotherapies have promoted the interests of the individual over the collective and have supported self-control over what Sampson (1988) identified as "field control".

The concept of field control refers to the idea that meanings and outcomes of interactions are determined by the collective process rather than being the domain of autonomous individuals. Self-contained individualism has also been promoted by some of the family therapy models. The Bowenian model is a good example (Bowen, 1976, 1978). In spite of its emphasis on transgenerational patterns of family interaction, the Bowenian model emphasizes the differentiation and autonomy of the individual over the collective family experience. Bowenian theory emphasizes that the pinnacle of development is an autonomous, goal-directed, "being-for-self", rational individual. From the Bowenian perspective, the poorly differentiated person, the one who seeks love and approval, is "being for others", which emphasizes relatedness over self-interest. The poorly undifferentiated family is depicted as an amorphous collective mass from which the individual must differentiate and extract himself in order to be a "self" who can function in the world at large.

The family as a whole has, in many psychotherapy models, to fend for itself. This negative attitude towards the interdependent interests of the family continues to be reflected through the cultural emphasis on the separation of the self from what is negatively described as dependency. Dependency is something to be avoided. In fact, it has been our impression that we are a part of a society that is phobic and disdainful of dependency, at least as far as dominant males are concerned.

Our discomfort grew as we saw serious inequities practised by many individual psychotherapies. Among these inequities were blaming mothers while rationalizing the absence of fathers from family life; supporting adolescent separations at ever earlier ages; protecting the rights of the individual parent to divorce, while ignoring its impact on children and the rights of children to have voices in the process of family dissolution; valuing attributes associated with male gender over those associated with female gender; and the tendency of therapists to line up against the unseen parents, spouse, and/or children not present in the therapy—clients whom we refer to as our "shadow clients", the collective we affect without direct contact. Our concerns deepened as we worked with families, fractions of families, and individuals who were victims of those therapies deemed to be in the best interest of the individual, with little regard for the continuity of family relationships.

It is our distinct impression that those psychotherapies which emphasize the rights of the individual over the collective risk becoming a part of the problem rather than being part of the solution. Individualism, as a part of the politics of therapy, mirrors the politics of the larger society. Psychotherapists, some unwittingly, join the ranks of a political ideology that emphasizes the rights of the individual over the larger society. The psychotherapy fields could have seen individualism and the collective as complementary. But, as often happens in a typically dualistic society, these characteristics become adversarial. The psychotherapy movement is a political movement with a *cause célèbre*, the individual. These psychotherapists rescue the individual from the clutches of so-called pathological collectives: marriages, families, extended families, and communities. They act as warriors in a fight for the survival of individuals over the collective. They provide clients with sanctuary, a place of safety and comfort, a place where there is unconditional positive regard, and a place to plan their extrication from those who are depriving them of the freedom to be their "own self". Self becomes its own proscribed entity, not beholden to a context or ecology of relationships. Selfhood has no limits, no bounds. A psychological freedom. A given right.

Objectivity

From the beginning of our sojourn into psychotherapy, a particularly nettlesome idea kept gnawing at us: the notion of objectivity. Objectivity required us to intellectualize, rationalize, and otherwise distance ourselves from the emotional impact of the stories our clients told us about their lives. Could we really stand outside the experience of our clients' lives as they related them to us? Could we believe in the veracity of their stories without necessarily condoning them or sitting in judgement of them or of the other characters of their stories? Somewhere in the back of our minds we began to remember something that Martin Buber had said about listening to the story of others from what you imagine is the perspective of others and trying to understand their story from that perspective, yet not having to give up your own perspective in the bargain. He called this an act of inclusion (Buber, 1965a, p. 97). It was only a niggling of an idea at that point, but it would not go away.

Many of the texts we read, the seminar presenters we listened to, and the colleagues with whom we worked believed that therapists were chroniclers and codifiers of the negative attributes and deficits of individuals and families. They thought of themselves as professionals able to stand outside the experiences of their clients and receive these experiences dispassionately. They made observations and judgements from what they called an objective position. Therapists responded with professional distance to what they observed about clients. Clients transferred their subjective experiences onto an objective therapist. Therapists showed clients how they had transferred their perceptions of early relationships onto the therapist. The therapy then proceeded towards changing the negative attributes and deficits of those perceptions, which would then result in more satisfying experiences for the clients.

Countertransference

Countertransference from a traditional perspective was considered to be an interference with the objectivity of analysts. In the early days of psychoanalysis, countertransference was considered to be a troublesome phenomenon, one that interfered with the transference experience of the analysand (Menninger & Holzman, 1973). Freud recommended that one way of dealing with this interfering countertransference was for the analyst to remain aloof, unemotional, and detached like a surgeon (Freud, 1895). Countertransference had been thought to indicate that objectivity had been momentarily lost when therapists responded to clients from an emotional perspective, not a rational, dispassionate one. Later, analysts began to realize that psychoanalysis was "a two-party transactional relationship" (Menninger & Holzman, 1973). Nonetheless, it was still thought that therapists should strive to check their own subjective experiences at the door and leave them outside the therapy room in order to be objective. The continued suspicion and mistrust of countertransference as a useful experience among psychoanalysts is reflected in Menninger and Holzman's statement that, "one of the most important functions of psychoanalytic societies is a control of countertransference tendencies" (1973, p. 94). There remains a closely held belief in the necessity to be objective in order to concentrate exclusively on the experiences of the clients. What a comforting thought. What an invitation to feeling powerful and in control of the progress of the therapy. It was the true test of the personal discipline of self-contained, self-reliant, clear thinking psychotherapists. The psychotherapists had nothing personal at stake. It was all professional, objectifying, and rational. It was an example of how strongly we believe in the power of individuals who can discipline themselves to be in control of their feelings, prejudices, conflicts, and moods and stay outside the experience by concentrating on other persons. The psychotherapists were not in the experience, except for those few moments when they lost their objectivity. If they were aware of those moments, they could rectify the mistakes. If not, they could seek objective consultants or supervisors. What an invitation to hubris! It did not dawn on us until later that this could as easily be a prescription for doing harm as well as for doing good. Add to it the idea of confidentiality, and we have created the context and potential for doing harm in the name of doing good.

Psychotherapy and its traditions

Traditional psychotherapists (psychoanalysts, object relations psychotherapists, structural and strategic family therapists) come to therapy armed with maps of theory and practice to guide their interactions with clients. These interactions involve creating a match rather than a fit. Clients have to match the constructs and practices of the therapists, rather than therapists and clients creating a fit. Success or failure of therapy depends on how well clients match predetermined standards for successful change. We have always been uneasy with this orientation. This work requires distancing from others by objectifying them. The position of the authoritative knower did not fit for us. It is a critical example of where the scientific metaphor as a guide for how to conduct ourselves in relation to clients did not fit our experience of the way we were in the world. Our interest in constructing more equitable relationships with clients goes back to our days of philosophical and humanitarian studies. Buber and other philosophers continued to come to our conscious awareness as our discomfort with the habits and customs of applied science grew, until it became clear that using these traditional ideas was not ethical for us.

Therapists from the traditional disciplines give clinical, social, and political names to categories of behaviour. For example, such clinical names as character or personality disorders like the borderline personality, sociopathic character, and passive–aggressive personality are descriptors of behaviours that carry mostly negative tones and negatively connoted meanings. They are considered pathological states, deviations from norms. The therapists look for signs to confirm their diagnostic impressions, and they find it difficult to incorporate information that does not match predetermined categories. Psychotherapy is a fairly straightforward course for these psychotherapists, because they subscribe to the notion that clients should conform to a predetermined reality. The basic act of being clients puts people in a negatively connoted position. Therapists assume that clients are culpable for being different. The culpability flows from the client position. Clients are presumed to have something wrong with them or they would not be in the client position. The stigma attached to being in the client position is a circular one. Inherent in the name client is the presumption of pathology and deficit. This attitude creates distinctions, and social hierarchies follow from these distinctions. The dichotomous, hierarchical positions of client and therapist did not work for us. There by the grace of circumstances and context go we. Being in the client position did not mean being something lesser. Being therapists did not mean being something better. It meant that we were in a given context at a given moment in time.

As therapists we had to come to grips with the idea that we were as vulnerable to our preconceptions and organized belief systems as are clients. This compromises our ability to listen to the point of view of others. In order to practice in a manner that maintains continuity with our ethical perspective, we would have to make a shift in our attitude away from believing that our beliefs constitute the standard for conducting life and begin to listen to the point of view of others from our imagination of their point of view. The recognition of the need for this shift put us into a crisis of uncertainty. We had to acknowledge that knowing had to be changed from knowing based on preconceived notions of others to knowing being primarily imagining based on experiencing others in dialogue. This dialogue had to be based on a continual process of checking in with others about our experience of them and their experience of us, an ethical position that sets the stage for genuine dialogue and makes equity in relationships a given.

Many therapists find it difficult to accept the perspective of their clients as being as legitimate as their own. Therapists, like their clients, believe in their own constructions of reality. Therefore, "data fitting" is most likely to occur as the therapists interact with clients. Whatever clients say is put into pre-existing categories of meaning and used by therapists to confirm their theories about the clients. Naming, as a form of categorizing and attribution, helps diminish levels of uncertainty. Naming is a way of trying to bring certainty, stability, and objectivity into an interaction. Reliance on naming and objectivity, however, diminishes the possibility of engaging in a creative process that invites clients to contribute to the meanings evolved in the interaction.

We began to think that the idea of believing in objectivity was a false concept because it implied that the genuine self had to be held in abeyance, and from an ethical perspective that was impossible to do. We all bring our selfhood to bear on all our interpersonal contacts, professional or otherwise. Our self is our executive process, our way of making sense of our experience, and a way to organize our communication internally and externally. Only by using ourselves can we interact authentically and ethically and be truly in meeting or dialogue with clients. What we bring to any therapeutic encounter is who we believe we are as represented by a self. To the extent that therapists are not explorers of meanings but are collectors of data to match already existing categories, authentic interaction—for example, listening to the clients from an inclusive point of view—cannot take place. An inclusive point of view requires therapists to acknowledge the legitimacy of the perspective of others. Therapy can be a process of co-constructing meanings with clients, but such a process requires respect for the others' perspectives and consideration of them as legitimate in their own right.

CHAPTER THREE

Family therapy and change

Several years ago, as roving and naive cats, we wandered into the field of family therapy. We were intrigued and wanted to try it on for size. It showed such promise. It was just what the doctor ordered for two such knockabout, quick-change, tight-rope acrobats who were looking for something new to alleviate the feelings of uncertainty we had about our experiences in the field of individual psychotherapy. But, low and behold, it was the quick-change phenomenon that caught us up short in this new, pioneering field of family therapy.

American society's love affair with change, and the quicker the better, has led the field to participate in the deification of change as a way to salvation from the past and towards a better life in the future. It has been the justification for an aggressive mentality that promotes intrusive, invasive methods that belie an attitude of arrogance towards others. It has encouraged a belief in therapists as agents of change who have to have extraordinary powers to be clever enough to change families. Arrogance towards others and the deification of change serve as antidotes to the panic felt about the inability to control our lives, to say nothing of the lives of others.

It is a formidable task to buck such strong societal currents—ones that honour aggressive methods and the push to get the job done, never mind how. To not try to counteract that trend, however, means we will continue to be purveyors of those values that condone power, control, and hierarchical position. Furthermore, our ability to relate effectively to how these values impact on gender, generation, race, and poverty, and the role of physiognomy in relationships, will be diminished.

The more familiar we became with the field of family therapy, the more we discovered its fascination with bringing about change rather than with other constructs like healing (Friedman, 1985; Inger & Inger, 1990a), coherence (Dell, 1982), gender, and generativity (Goldner, 1988). It has produced a plethora of strategies, interventions, prescriptions (variant and invariant), solutions, miracles, and other beguiling notions designed to further the mission of changing others. This preoccupation with finding ways to change others has seemed to us arrogant and aggressive. It belies a lack of respect for the lifelong struggles of clients. It is devoid of compassion for others. The desire to change others stems from an ideology of blame and disapproval for the way others live their lives, and it implies a process of judging others. Therapists who set out to change others put themselves in a higher position in the social order than the ones they are judging. Putting therapists in the judgement chair can be dangerous. It puts them in the position of interpreting and representing the interests of society over the interests of the clients. In some ways we felt right back where we started from in the old neighbourhood of individual psychotherapy with its language and practices about changing the internal, negative attributes of clients. Our instincts as aesthetic cats was to mistrust these practical applications of changing others by virtue of our clever acts and acrobatic ability to walk a paradoxical tightrope across the abyss of change for the sake of making a difference.

Family therapy as a social and economic movement has been fascinated with change and seduced by charismatic therapists with theories about change borrowed from the physical and biological sciences, by cultural fads, and by market-place pressures to produce quick and cheap solutions. As one of the newer forms of psychotherapy, family therapy has had to prove its efficacy, its value to the mental health movement. It could not simply compete with the established psychotherapies. It had to have a better mouse-trap. The traditional psychotherapies were based on a process that claimed to produce continuous changes within the individual over long periods of time. Individuals were believed to operate on the principle that internal psychological changes must be congruent with the various interdependent components of the psychological structure called self or ego. To help an individual change, therapists and the individuals had to find ways to make new or transformed components fit the existing interdependent whole. Changes had to be compatible with the integrity of the existing psychological struc-ture of the individual. But no attention was paid to how the changes of the individual did or did not integrate with the patterns of inter-actions among the individuals who form the units of interaction, like families. Nor was attention paid to the potential reactions of others to the changes of the individual, and the impact of those reactions on the individual.

Discontinuous change is a different matter. Discontinuous change is more likely to occur in a group than within individuals. Inducing discontinuous change by interrupting the current interactional coherence of the family is a common practice in family therapy. That interruption can destroy the old interactional coher-ence, but a new coherence is sure to ensue from the interactions. Bateson (1979) called this a self-healing tautology. He warned, how-ever, that this self-healing process is unpredictable (Bateson, 1979, p. 206).

Long-lasting change is not easy to produce in individuals through methods that promote discontinuous change. Therefore, individual members within the family are not necessarily expected to change through the process of family therapy (Dell, 1982). Change is expected to take place at the level of interaction among family members. Continuous change of the family as a whole takes too long, so it is not very popular. Family therapy carved out a niche by claiming to produce discontinuous change in less time. The fascination with discontinuous change and the need to be brief has encouraged more aggressive methods, ones that are designed to produce particular ends. Time has become something to manipu-late, something to change in itself. So family therapists have played with the perceptions of time and how to use it to change interactional patterns between individuals and within families

(Boscolo & Bertrando, 1993). This fascination has distracted us from reflecting on ourselves as therapists and our contributions to the therapeutic experience.

Family therapy has swung far away from the individual towards an emphasis on the collective in its view of the family as a system. As a result, the field has lost sight of the importance of the complementarity between the individuals and the family as a collective, and of the fact that both must be considered. There is an irony about this dichotomous position because the field as a whole promotes individual "master therapists" over the collective bodies of families. Workshops, conferences, and annual meetings of the various family therapy organizations are a good example of how the "master therapist" is promoted as someone who has extraordinary individual powers to produce change with families as collective bodies.

One way we have addressed the problem of the individual and the collective as it relates to families and therapists is by using a team approach (Inger & Inger, 1990a, 1990b). Although most teams have one therapist in the therapy room, we find that using two therapists in the room as co-therapists relates to the problem of the tensions between individualism and collectivity as well as problems of arrogance. It relates to gender issues, since we are a male and a female, and allows us to relate to adversarial problems by each reflecting one side of an issue and together discussing differences, making distinctions, and talking about options. This reflecting process between co-therapists allows the family reflective distance from issues, presents new perspectives, and provides the family enough safety to become more flexible in their approach to problems. In this way we, as co-therapists, can present these different perspectives to the family through our reflections to each other and shed new light on the tensions produced by the competing interests of the individuals and the family. As a co-therapy team, we have the advantage of being able to take "both . . . and . . ." positions. The potential for arrogance is diminished as we assume complementary positions, thus demonstrating that there is no one right position and there is no one right answer.

CHAPTER FOUR

Evolving an ethic of being

Objectivity, a required attitude in traditional psychotherapies, had been constraining our propensity to be compassionate in our work. We found ourselves returning to our earlier interest in philosophical thinking and genuine dialogue. We dusted off our Buber books and familiarized ourselves with his thinking about human relationships. We discovered that central to Buber's thinking is the notion that a person is never alone in the world. He or she is always in relation to another or others. How we participate in that relationship differs depending upon our attitude towards ourselves and others.

According to Buber, a genuine dialogue requires us to imagine the experience of another from that other's perspective while maintaining our own perspective. Buber used the phrase "imagining the real" to describe the act of committing oneself fully to putting oneself "into the life of the Other" (1965b, p. 81). Imagining the real is how we think of the other when we make that person known to ourselves. Imagining another from that perspective is what Buber describes as an act of inclusion (1965a, p. 97). Acting from an attitude of inclusion occurs when one (as in the case of psychotherapy

21

or teaching) or both (as in the case of friendship and love) persons take the position of the other in order to imagine what the other is experiencing, feeling, intending, thinking, and believing. At the same time, the person who is practising inclusion does not give up their own feelings, beliefs, thoughts, or intentions. The attitude of inclusion constitutes accepting both one's own and the other's point of view as legitimate (Inger, 1993). This idea transforms the traditional concept of countertransference from an essentially negative idea about an internal emotional state experienced by therapists to a concept that encourages therapists to take both the client's and their own perspectives into account. In spite of attempts to alter the idea of countertransference as a negative attribute, there remains the idea that countertransference is an indicator that objectivity has been lost, rather than seeing that countertransference can add richness to the contact between therapists and clients. This mistrust of countertransference belies a basic mistrust among therapists about therapists' intentions and motives towards clients, especially those that they believe to emanate from the so-called unconscious, an internal state that therapists seem to mistrust in themselves and in their clients.

Ideas from the world of philosophy in the past several years have come to form the foundation for our work, a foundation that allows us to legitimize our feelings of compassion for clients. This kind of thinking has been an avenue for moving away from the constraining rules of traditional psychotherapies and their insistence on predetermined meanings, towards an ethically based psychotherapy that elevates the relational aspects to a place of prominence and promotes co-created meanings.

What experiences might move therapists into a position of being self-reflective and sensitive to the legitimacy of both their own positions and those of others? There is perceived personal and societal power in being in a position of objectivity. Judges enjoy a very elevated status in society when they perform duties thought to reflect their ability to be objective. Many therapists enjoy a similar position of power, since the perception of therapists as objective knowers still exists and remains seductive. A status hard to relinquish. Objectivity requires a sense of dualism, either this or that, right or wrong, and other finite possibilities. Self-reflectivity

requires a sense of relativity, both this and that, and infinite possibilities and uncertainties. It connotes a view of the world as a place
where contraries are reconciled, not resolved. Unity is found in the
reconciliation of differences and not in the destruction of differences. What makes the difference between persons who take the
stance of objectivity and persons who go beyond objectivity to see
themselves as part of a co-constructing experience and meaning-
making ecology? We obviously do not know the answer, but we
have found others in different fields who have transformed their
beliefs under difficult or extreme circumstances, and who have been
able to take self-reflective postures about those transformations.

A crisis of uncertainty is one in which the existing world view of
the person no longer works for him, and his doubts pile up to the
point of demanding a change in attitude and action. Crises of uncertainty are internal and personal; thus accounts of such crises are
anecdotal descriptions of inner turmoil. Issues of personal beliefs
clash with new ideas that have come about from unusual experiences and cannot be reconciled with the old beliefs. The crisis
centres on how to reconcile these two competing world views and
transform them into a new whole that makes sense.

Part of the solace we gained during times of uncertainty about
our beliefs and practices and how we could reconcile conflicting
beliefs was hearing and reading about how others dealt with crises
of uncertainty as they struggled with the world of ideas and practices. It was comforting. We learned much from the ways in which
others framed their dilemmas and went about the reconciliations
and transformative experiences. We could identify their pain and
ours and see the similarities and differences in their experiences
when confronted with the unmistakable demands for changing
views and practices. In the spirit of the value of shared experiences,
we offer three examples of crises of uncertainty. These ideas, drawn
from diverse sources, broaden the premises of our own beliefs. The
experiences of others have served the purpose of illuminating the
many potentials of human experience, bringing us face to face with
issues we might find easy to overlook or ignore. Dramatists, anthro-
pologists, and philosophers have been rich sources of ideas. They
differentiate themselves from applied scientists by disclaiming
a belief in objectivity. They speak from their own carefully con-

structed world views. They reflect an ethic of being that is different from that proffered by many traditional psychotherapists.

We have chosen three persons, each representing different perspectives, who articulate the experience they have had of turning to their own internal resources to guide them through a painful process of profoundly changing their beliefs. These examples give us some insight about how ethical perspectives can evolve. The three have several themes in common, including a basic reliance on one's ability to handle ambiguity and uncertainty, a commitment to seeing an experience through in spite of the pain and tension of uncertainty, and a faith in one's own ability to cope with novelty and unforeseen circumstances.

The first person is the fictional character Dr. Richard Dysart of the play *Equus* by British playwright, Peter Shaffer (1974). The second person is the philosophical anthropologist Martin Buber, and the third person is the Norwegian family therapist Tom Andersen. They are examples of persons who have come face to face with painful internal and interpersonal issues, and they have stayed with the tension of uncertainty long enough to transform it into new belief systems. Each has devoted a great deal of his life's work to the concept of subjectivity in all its genuineness. As one shifts away from a belief in an objectifiable world, one has to let go of time-honoured external props like categorical thinking, hierarchy, and reliance on absolutes. It is like moving from a comfortable old armchair onto a three-legged stool. We have to rely on our own subjective perceptions, and we have to use our "selves" in ways heretofore not considered by traditional psychotherapies.

A FICTIONAL CHARACTER'S CRISIS OF BELIEFS

In the play *Equus* (Shaffer, 1974), Dr. Richard Dysart, a child psychiatrist, is confronted with a situation that rocks the foundation of his beliefs and practices. He is faced with the failure of his professional beliefs to see him through a very taxing therapeutic situation with Alan, an adolescent who has been hospitalized for violently putting out the eyes of horses in a sexually ritualized manner. Dr. Dysart is not prepared for what he encounters with this boy. His mental network of theoretical cause-and-effect explanations does not serve him in this extreme case. He cannot explain to himself how this boy can become what he seems to have become, and he cannot separate himself from the experience with which this boy is burdened. As we shall read below, Dr. Dysart is in danger of losing his "objectivity". He, like many mental health professionals, believes in objectivity as a shibboleth of his work. As the play unfolds, he comes to the point in his life where he can no longer refuse to acknowledge the legitimacy of the reality of another from that other's world view in spite of the grotesqueness of that view. Because the reality of the boy is constructed from genuine experience and woven together into an intricate metaphor from fragments of experiences, the violent incident that personifies the unity of those fragments throws Dr. Dysart into a crisis about the legitimacy of his own beliefs and practices and the foundation upon which they are constructed. He no longer derives comfort from the notion that the boy is simply psychotic, mentally ill, or pathological. Dr. Dysart is confronted with the agony of an experience of extreme self-doubt and the prospect of being in a position of not knowing.

> Dysart: The thing is, I'm desperate. You see, I'm wearing that horse's head myself. That's the feeling. All reined up in old language and old assumptions, straining to jump clean-hoofed on to a whole new track of being I only suspect is there. I can't see it, because my educated, average head is being held at the wrong angle. I can't jump because the bit forbids it, and my own basic force—my horsepower, if you like—is too little. The only thing I know for sure is this: a horse's head is finally unknowable to me. Yet I handle children's heads—which I must presume to be more complicated, at least in the area of my chief concern. . . . The doubts have been there for years, piling up steadily in this dreary place. It's only the extremity of this case that's made them active. I know that. The *extremity* is the point! [p. 22]

Let us tease out some of the implications of what Dr. Dysart strains to tell us in his soliloquy. It is a poignant reflection of a crisis of uncertainty. Dr. Dysart articulates the dilemma we face when treating other human beings. We all wear some of the characteristics of our clients. We are bound up in our professional jargon and other forms of categorical thinking, interpretation, and explanation.

The theoretical and practical "bit" often forbids, or at least constrains, us from being creative and experimental. The "bit" of our beliefs constrains our thinking and acting, and, as the "bit" cuts into our flesh, it holds us back from being spontaneous or intuitive about how we want to act and respond. The "bit", as it constrains us, reminds us of how well we have learned our professional beliefs and rituals and how well trained we are at constraining ourselves against the risk of spontaneity and creativity. We have all come away from therapeutic encounters bemoaning our temporary inability to be knowers—that is, able to say we know the other concretely as the other. Yet we hang on tenaciously to the belief that we are knowers. It is just that we do not momentarily know that particular client or family. The basic ability to know, however, is not abandoned. Not yet. On the other hand, through experience we feel the piling up of our doubts, our uncertainties, and our misgivings about the efficacy of what we are doing as therapists and how we go about it. This dilemma, expressed by Dr. Dysart, comes from epistemological assumptions about how the world of relationships works and how we participate in that relational world. For instance, we believe we must remain separate, distant, and bending away from our clients rather than being in mutuality with them, bridging distances of meaning and bending towards them.

In his encounter at the emotional extreme, Dr. Dysart is both appalled and fascinated by this boy who created a ritual with horses to act out a set of fantasies that, based on fragments of experiences, propelled him into violent, sexual action. The fantasies, as they collected into a whole metaphor, made demands on him to express himself in ways that were beyond his control. The internal tension between being fascinated and appalled led Dr. Dysart into a tortuous experience of restructuring his personal and professional epistemology by entering the uncharted waters of imagining his patient's realm of thinking, acting, and being. He propelled himself into the boy's perspective rather than his own. He wore the horse's head himself, found his own language noticeably useless as he sweated and strained to jump into a whole new track of being. But he was caught up short by the "bit" of a traditional categorical meaning system, and he concludes that the horse's head is unknowable to him because he would have to throw off the old "bit", the old constraints, in order to devote himself to the reality of the patient. He would have to suspend his own reality in order to try to imagine the patient's perspective and be inclusive with him. This truly is a formidable task. It requires a suspension of judgement—a suspension of categories of belief long enough to appreciate the other as the other in his own right. This puts each and both in a state of mutuality of being as opposed to a state of seeming. It creates relationship rather than distance. The state of being is characterized by giving oneself spontaneously to the other without regard for the impression one is making on the other. Therefore, the relationship is based on the authenticity of the spontaneity of those in relationship. The state of seeming, on the other hand, is characterized by a concern for what the other thinks of him, which is indicative of a wish for approval or confirmation from the other as the primary motive for being in that relationship (Friedman, 1985, p. 121; Buber, 1965b, pp. 75–78).

Dr. Dysart confronts himself when he reveals to himself that the horse's head is unknowable to him. This sense of unknowing leads him to face the doubts that have been piling up in his mind for years. It was this extreme situation that catapulted Dr. Dysart into a critical look at and re-evaluation of his assumptions about general knowledge as against local knowledge. In his quest for local knowledge, Dr. Dysart went to Alan's family home and allowed the bits and pieces of the story to take a new shape outside of the gestalt of cause-and-effect psychology. He had to leave behind the quest for objectivity and social control, the usefulness of social hierarchical structures, and the act of naming (e.g. diagnosing) to ensure certainty and stability. He had to give up the idea of being an autonomous being, objectively interacting with another but untouched by the other. He fell into a state of being characterized by knowing the other from the point of view of the other. This was itself a terrorizing experience for Dr. Dysart, and he eventually fell back into the more comfortable state of objectification, but no longer arrogantly. He would always have some doubt of himself and of his knowing.

After all the internal pain and suffering Dr. Dysart went through to try to change his beliefs, he ended up treating his patient, Alan, in a traditional manner, restoring him to so-called normalcy so that

Alan would no longer feel the pain that drove him to sexually violent acts. But what about Dr. Dysart's pain? He speaks to that question in the following way.

> Dysart: And now for me it never stops: that voice of Equus out of the cave—"Why Me? . . . Why Me? . . . Account for Me! . . . All right—I surrender! I say it . . . In an ultimate sense I cannot know what I do in this place—yet I do ultimate things. Essentially I cannot know what I do—yet I do essential things. Irreversible, terminal things. I stand in the dark with a pick in my hand, striking at heads! I need—more desperately than my children need me—a way of seeing in the dark. What way is this? . . . *What dark is this?* . . . I cannot call it ordained of God: I can't get that far. I will however pay it so much homage. There is now, in my mouth, this sharp chain. And it never comes out. [p. 125]

This is the sharp chain of constraints. It is the constraints of social convention. It is the constraints experienced when doing what is necessary for the greater good, and the constraints we feel when we know the treatment may harm the spirit of the person treated, when we believe that the greater good was served but the individual was not served. That is the sharp chain. It is discomforting to those who reflect on the question of whom we represent—the person or family we treat, or the social and economic system that pays us? What is the point of our treatment? Who is ultimately and essentially served? Dr. Dysart struggles with this question and concludes that he cannot see in this dark place, but short of seeing in dark places he knows he has a chain in his mouth like the well-trained horse. The chain serves as a reminder of the constraints on our creative abilities, our freedom to know intuitively, and our ability to go against the cultural prescriptions that are embedded in us all the time.

A PHILOSOPHICAL ANTHROPOLOGIST'S CRISIS OF UNCERTAINTY

Martin Buber first identified the concepts of I–Thou and I–It as primary relational modes, as well as related concepts of mutuality and genuine dialogue (1958, 1965a, 1965b, 1973). He shares an experience with us in *Between Man and Man* (1965a), which concerns his first encounter, at age 11, with what later became known as an I–Thou relationship. Oddly enough, it concerned an encounter with a horse. It was a transforming experience for him as a youth, but its import only became clear later in his life.

> When I was eleven years of age, spending the summer on my grandparents' estate, I used, as often as I could do it unobserved, to steal into the stable and gently stroke the neck of my darling, a broad dapple-gray horse. It was not a casual delight but a great, certainly friendly, but also deeply stirring happening. If I am to explain it now, beginning from the still very fresh memory of my hand, I must say that what I experienced in touch with the animal was the Other, the immense otherness of the Other. . . . When I stroked the mighty mane, sometimes marvelously smooth-combed, at other times just as astonishingly wild, and felt the life beneath my hand, it was as though the element of vitality itself bordered on my skin, something that was not I, was certainly not akin to me, palpably the other, not just another, really the Other itself; and yet it let me approach, confided itself to me, placed itself elemental in the relation of *Thou* and *Thou* to me. [pp. 22–23]

Here we find that the seminal experience of Buber's philosophy, the I–Thou relationship, occurred in an encounter with a horse. It was not an intellectual or verbal connection. The I–Thou connection was kinaesthetic. It took place between Buber's hand and the body of the horse. The feeling of unity or oneness for Buber, like Alan, the boy in *Equus*, took place without words. Horses confirmed both Buber and Alan. The horse stirred Buber, and he remembered it in his hand. Mind, the essential connectedness between oneself and the other, is not exclusively in the brain. I–Thou connectedness is not simply between or among people. Buber provides us with the idea that I–Thou connectedness is not only possible with all living things, but that an I–Thou connectedness is sensual, non-verbal, and not intellectual. It is intuitive, kinaesthetic, concrete, a product of the moment. A product of the *between* that is created mutually among beings in relation to one another.

Buber also taught about the essential nature of the I–It relationship and the fact that the I–It attitude is likewise an essential mode of relationship. In the same context and with the same horse, he had his first realization of an I–It relationship. He states:

But once—I do not know what came over the child, at any rate it was childlike enough—it struck me about the stroking, what fun it gave me, and suddenly I became conscious of my hand. The game went on as before, but something had changed, it was no longer the same thing. And the next day, after giving him a rich feed, when I stroked my friend's head he did not raise his head. [p. 23]

Buber realized that he had treated the horse as an object by focusing on his own pleasure of stroking it. Buber had changed his attitude towards the horse from one of a being who was his friend to that of a being who was the object of his pleasure. This allowed Buber to recognize the twofold nature of relationships—the I–It and the I–Thou. Both are an essential part of living in relationships. Buber insisted that without It humans cannot live, but the person who lives with I–It relationships at the extreme cannot be fully human (Buber, 1958). The world of It is the world of information and facts. The world of Thou is the world of relations, the world of the present among persons.

Buber also experienced a personal crisis of uncertainty, which caused a major shift in his thinking and acting. This crisis led him to bring together the spiritual life and the everyday life through concrete experiencing. Prior to the experience described below, Buber was devoted to his religious practices as if they were separate from the ordinary activities of daily life. Through a crisis of uncertainty he came to believe that his religious ideas had to fit into the context of everyday living. The impetus to change those ideas did, however, take an experience at the extreme. It was the death of another person that put him into a crisis of uncertainty which led to a radical change in his philosophy, religious practices, and approach to relational life. Buber's crisis of uncertainty reminds us of Dr. Dysart's soliloquy and, as we shall see, of Tom Andersen's slow but sure move towards a more syntonic way of being a family therapist in his own culture.

Buber tells us:

... after a morning of "religious" enthusiasm, I had a visit from an unknown young man, without being there in spirit. I conversed attentively and openly with him—only I omitted to guess the questions which he did not put. Later, not long after, I learned from one of his friends—he himself was no longer alive—the essential content of these questions; I learned that he had come to me not casually, but borne by destiny, not for a chat but for a decision. He had come to me; he had come in this hour. What do we expect when we are in despair and yet go to a man? Surely, a presence by means of which we are told that nevertheless there is meaning. Since then I have given up the "religious" which is nothing but the exception, extraction, exaltation, ecstasy; or it has given me up. I possess nothing but the everyday out of which I am never taken. [1965a, pp. 13–14]

As the above story from Buber's life indicates, he had an uprooting experience at the extreme. Buber had been paying more attention to his own religious ecstasy than to the present when the young man came seeking a decision. Not to have been in the present when meeting with this man did not allow him to experience the man's pain and, hence, potential for death. Buber found out later from the young man's friend that there was nothing in the young man that opposed his own death. In battle, the man did not try to save himself. The man's death changed Buber's way of thinking about his relationship to others. His reflection upon not having been in the moment and its consequences led Buber to move away from the abstractions of his spirituality towards attending to the concrete moment as the essence of being. His life represented an ethic of being fully in the present. This experience taught Buber that his spirituality was to be found in the everyday relationship between himself and others in which there is a sense of shared responsibility in dialogue. The between is their social construction, their creation. Not all meetings are alike. Buber distinguishes one that he called "genuine dialogue". By genuine dialogue he emphasized that the dialogue has value in itself and not as a means to another end.

According to Buber, how we enter a dialogue will, in part, determine its direction. Like the social constructionists (Berger & Luckman, 1966; Gergen, 1985), Buber believes that a person's experience forms the basis for his relationship to the external world. He believes that the participants co-construct the dialogic experience based on one of two attitudes they can invoke in that dialogue. The twofold attitude is I–It and I–Thou. Each participant in the dialogic context is continually making distinctions and decisions about how to act and how to regard the other and how he is regarded by the other as well. These attitudinal distinctions also lead to various constraints and eventually to patterns of attitudes and interactions in the dialogue.

A FAMILY THERAPIST'S CRISIS
WITH CULTURAL DISCONTINUITY

Tom Andersen, the Norwegian family therapist, relates his experience of using and eventually transforming an objectifying set of methods of family therapy which did not fit into his culture or soothe the tension of his intuition, all of which put him into a prolonged state of uneasiness. Andersen (1991) takes us on a journey through the processes he and his team followed on their way to inventing the reflecting team. He tells us about the values of the Norwegian culture regarding relationships and how he realized that his culture required him to be more modest when interacting with families than his more flamboyant and charismatic American and Italian counterparts. He explains how his culture constrained and augmented the creative process, and the combination of timidity and courage they experienced in trying new methods. After three years of struggling with ideas, the reflecting-team notion was ready for application. So it was with uncertainty and humility that they put it into practice.

> I had been struggling with some ideas for two or three years together with my co-therapist (Aina Skorpen, MHN), but a lack of courage prevented me from bringing the ideas to light. . . .
> It took us three years before we dared to let them see us work. . . .
> So this idea had a long gestation period.
> One day, however, in March 1985, the idea pushed for a birth. [p. 11]

One of the most interesting aspects of the development or invention of the reflecting team is Andersen's reminiscences about his own experience of what pushed him into radically altering the ways in which he and his team conducted family therapy. In his book, Andersen discusses his feelings of uneasiness about the work of the team and how that uneasiness did not go away (p. 162). He continues his reminiscence about his feeling of uneasiness:

> What has been interesting . . . has been noticing that the feeling of uneasiness in various relationships has stimulated major changes in the way I work. Actually, all the changes mentioned above come from such wonderings about feeling uneasy. What is the basis for that feeling of being uneasy in a relationship? While I have no "objective" answer to that, I have devoted much thought to it. [p. 163]

His was not uneasiness at the extreme, but rather a continuing state of uneasiness that would not go away. The uneasiness seemed to have to do with the hierarchical position of the therapists in relation to the families. The therapists were uneasy about being authoritative and hierarchical because it went against Norwegian cultural beliefs and practices. The practice of reflecting with the family as opposed to delivering an intervention to the family made local sense to them and allowed them to be more consistent with their cultural values and mores. This transformed way of doing family therapy allowed the team to remain syntonic with the cultural belief about the proper way of relating and, yet, effective in providing just enough difference to give the families impetus to move towards change that made sense to them.

The reflecting team came into existence with some of the drama one would expect in a struggle for change. It was not a cold, calculated invention of applied science. On the contrary, it was a rather intense, culturally prescribed drama about meaning and social contact among participants to an exchange of ideas and ways of communicating. One could speculate that the demands of local knowledge prevailed over generalized knowledge, and imported methods of intervening eventually gave way to the reflecting team. The reflecting-team method altered the uncomfortable format of an authoritative hierarchy, which included the hiding of information. The Italian and American formats were too aggressive and arrogant for this culture. In one creative swoop, Andersen and his team solved the problem of feeling uneasy. Only later did they search for a rationale beyond their local knowledge to try to communicate to others the possible meanings and significance of what they did. Tom Andersen (1991) now feels he should not try so hard to offer explanations. Yet, there is intense external pressure from the field to explain what this reflecting team's perturbation means to the field so that others can generalize and use it. We feel we must value the perturbation for what it means to those who invented it in a particular context under specific conditions and not generalize a universal meaning. To make the reflecting team a mechanical method is to lose its significance as a transactional movement from a state of seeming to a state of being that allowed the group to be in an authentic conversation among themselves and with families.

We must remember that the Andersen team's ideas incubated over a prolonged period of time, similar to those of the Milan team (Selvini-Palazzoli, Boscolo, Cecchin, & Prata, 1978). Both were being syntonic with their cultural values, beliefs, and practices. The Andersen team has shared some of the details of their struggle to invent a reflecting team that could work with families in a format of give and take, including mutual listening and genuine dialogue. To believe that the methods from one specific culture can be transported in their entirety across cultures is to miss the very point of social construction thinking. The Andersen team cogently points out that changing their practice with families required an adherence to their cultural context as well as to the creative process (Andersen, 1991).

Another element to the social construction process was Andersen's description of his conceptualization of the change that gave birth to the reflecting team. This is the legitimization of the internal experience of intuition.

> Intuition is in my terms a state of being open to the "answers" from "inside" myself when I am "touched" from "outside". [p. 164]

Andersen describes the changes he experienced as he and the team moved towards genuine dialogue with families. He talks about opening up to the outside when struggling for answers from inside himself. It is a struggle to be able to listen simultaneously to the voice from inside (intuition) and the voices from outside (receptive listening). That could be seen as a state of being present in the moment of dialogic exchange. The reflecting team is a personification of an attempt to approach a state of being present in a social exchange rather than maintaining a state of seeming to be in contact with the family. Andersen himself describes the struggle to get to that position. He cannot adequately describe its origins to himself, possibly because, as Buber indicates, you can prepare for an I–Thou relationship but you cannot make it happen. It seems to happen out of a state of "grace" (Buber, 1958, p. 11).

THREE EXPERIENCES
OF UNCERTAINTY SUMMARIZED

These three experiences have been transforming for each of the three people—the fictional therapist, the family therapist, and the philosophical anthropologist. Their crises of uncertainty brought about considerable tension and would not abate until the beliefs and practices based on certainty had transformed into beliefs and actions that incorporated uncertainty as an expected state of being. In the case of Dr. Dysart, he came to know that his treatment of the boy could not be based on old, traditional practices if he was to save the life spirit of the boy. Dysart had to live with his angst about his beliefs and treatment methods of social control. Tom Andersen knew that the way he and his team had been doing family therapy was somehow dystonic and incompatible with the beliefs and practices of his culture, and the way in which people went about the business of relating to one another. He introduced uncertainty into his work through the method of spontaneous, unrehearsed reflecting by the team. Martin Buber realized that his religious practices kept him outside the realm of the present and separated him from the other so that a genuine dialogue could not take place. As long as he separated the temporal from the religious, he would be left outside the moment of the dialogue which is essential in an interhuman exchange. Buber acknowledged that uncertainty is part of any dialogic encounter and a necessary component of an I–Thou relationship.

CHAPTER FIVE

Practising
from an ethical perspective

Psychotherapy, as reflective of philosophical thinking, was not a subject of much concern in the psychotherapy literature nor was it represented in methods of practice except for a few practitioners like Frankl (1959), who concerned himself with psychotherapy as a search for meanings. As we delved deeper into the differences between philosophical and scientific thinking, we discovered, along with many other family therapists and theorists, that many scientists were struggling with very similar concerns about objectivity, subjectivity, observers, and the observed. Some of the notions of the philosophy of science (e.g. Maturana, 1978; Von Foerster, 1981; Capra, 1982; Von Glasersfeld, 1979, 1984) were being introduced into the family therapy field. At the same time, some family therapists were becoming interested in the process of therapy rather than the content of therapy, especially the focus on the contributions of the therapists to the culture of therapy (to cite a few examples: Keeney, 1983; Watzlawick, 1984; Segal, 1986; Boscolo, Cecchin, Hoffman, & Penn, 1987). The main element of concern seemed to be centred around Von Foerster's (1981) thinking that we must bring observers into the experiences observed.

There can be no separation between the experiences of the observers and what they report to observe. They are a part of the same experience. We learn as much about the observers who report experiences as we do about the so-called reality of the experiences. Just what particulars are needed to legitimize that point of view in the actual practices of psychotherapy?

It was Keeney's (1983) observation that, as we look beyond the dualism of objectivity and subjectivity, we run headlong into the alternative, ethics. From this position beyond the gestalt of applied science, we come face to face with, "the necessary connection of the observer with the observed, which leads to examining *how* the observer participates in the observed" (Keeney, 1983, p. 80).

How we, as therapists, participate "in the observed" is the nexus of an ethical foundation for family therapy. It speaks to an intimate participation in therapy on the part of therapists. This idea of the observer and observed has a history that goes back before the time of Plato and his "Allegory of the Cave", in which he calls into question a belief in an absolute reality as it applies to all persons in a given context.

The tradition in applied science was to ignore the question of the influence of the observer on the observed. Scientists invoked the principle of objectivity, which was supposed to exempt them from undue influence on their subjects of study. It was Polyani (1969), a philosopher of science, who initially caught our attention as he wrote about the problems of objectivity and human responsibility in science.

> No, a humanistic revisionism can be secured only by revising the claims of science itself. The first task must be to emancipate the biological sciences, including psychology, from the scourge of physicalism; the absurdities now imposed on the sciences of life must be eliminated. The task is difficult, for it calls in question an ideal of impersonal objectivity on which alone we feel it safe to rely. Yet this absurd ideal must be discarded. And if once we succeed in this, we shall find that science no longer threatens man's responsible existence. [p. 46]

Belief in objectivity implies that it will always lead practitioners of science in the direction of justifiable and responsible behaviour as long as they follow the principles of science. Polyani spoke of that as a paradox: that objectivity, like certainty, creates the illusion of safety. He sees objectivity as the oppressor of science and of man's responsible existence. Objectivity cannot lead scientists in the direction of safety, but it can lead them to doing harm. It was Bateson (Bateson & Bateson, 1987) who stated an unequivocal mistrust for the motives of applied scientists. He believed that they stood to gain personally by their efforts; therefore, they could not claim dispassion or objectivity. This meant to us that, at the same time that traditional psychotherapists were using objectivity as an antidote for doing harm in their work, philosophers were seeing objectivity itself as a concept that could lead to doing harm in all areas of applied science.

It was believed by scientists that objectivity was a protection against abusing the power of science. If the scientist was objective, then he could not be corrupted. However, that myth does not take into account the essential humanness of the scientist, his vulnerability to using power that is not necessarily in everyone's best interest. No one is exempt from the abuse of power. The issue of power is inherent in all relationships. The animal kingdom has natural checks and balances on power. Hierarchy is based on strength, camouflage, speed, and cunning. When we look at the artificial checks and balances that we have developed for dealing with power for our civilized cultures, we find that the antidotes to power are also illusions.

Having given up a belief in objectivity, we were face to face with a universal question of power. Assuming that power is potential in all relationships and that we do not get rid of power issues in relationships *ipso facto*, one of the crucial issues therapists must think about in relation to their clients is how they use and potentially misuse power. Even though power may be thought of as a myth or a social and political construction, it is, according to Bateson (1972),

> . . . a very powerful myth and probably most people in the world more or less believe in it. It is a myth which, if everybody believes in it, becomes to that extent self-validating. [p. 486]

Psychotherapy has the potential for becoming a hierarchical relationship based on power. Clients come seeking relief from pain from those they presume know how to relieve that pain. This creates an inherent inequality in the therapeutic relationship. How we deal with or do not deal with it in psychotherapy becomes a part of the culture of that psychotherapy. From an ethically based perspective, power must be acknowledged as a part of the relationships among therapists, among family members, and between therapists and families. When basing therapy on ethical principles, power becomes one of the legitimate topics for dialogue in psychotherapy.

The use of persuasion, language, recourse to social control, and the like are power issues that are of major concern when considering the question of doing good or doing harm. The way the use of power unfolds in psychotherapy depends on the way therapists process their internal experience in their encounters with clients. Once again we have found ourselves probing outside our field to find guidance about how to understand the complexity of these philosophical dilemmas we face as psychotherapists. Hannah Arendt (1977), in *The Life of the Mind*, was concerned with the question of whether it is possible to abstain from evil-doing, which is analogous to the questions therapists must ask about whether they can abstain from doing harm to their clients. She queries,

> Could the activity of thinking as such, the habit of examining whatever happens to come to pass or to attract attention, regardless of results and specific content, could this activity be among the conditions that make men abstain from evil-doing or even actually "condition" them against it? [p. 5]

Arendt poses a question that is central to an ethical perspective for therapists. She asks whether the act of thinking about ourselves and our work through self-scrutiny can function to aid us in abstaining from doing harm. Self-scrutiny is a conscious process of reflecting on our thoughts and actions. It requires conscious attending to and valuing both. Self-reflective articulation is the sharing of our thinking about our clients with our clients. It requires a nonjudgemental posture and a "both . . . and . . ." position relative to the issues brought to the therapy. When we can no longer follow a repetitious how-to map for psychotherapists, then we will become aware of the moment-to-moment reflectivity in our own thinking and have less concern for judging the content of our clients' thoughts and lives.

As we have established, therapy with families means we are in an experience of mutual influence. It means that we have to attend to the authenticity of that experience. We cannot allow ourselves to stand outside of the experience and pretend it will not impact on us. This position requires that we consider the value and meaning of the experience to the family and to ourselves simultaneously. We find that when we put ourselves in the place of our clients and imagine ourselves to be the recipients of our own questions and actions, we are invoking the concept of inclusion, thus creating an ethical position (Buber, 1965a).

Philosophical thinking affords us the opportunity to be interested in the nature of knowing, the contributions of the knower to the experience of knowing; consequently, it demands a self-reflective position about the experience of knowing. A philosophical position requires us to acknowledge the limits of knowing, the limits of being in the knower position, and these limits allow for a context of not-knowing as opposed to the traditional requirement that therapists be knowers. Anderson and Goolishian (1988) have attempted to bring this notion into the fold of family therapy by suggesting that the work of therapists is managing the conversation without necessarily knowing where it is going or how it will turn out. This implies both being a knower of how to manage conversations and being a not-knower of how conversations will evolve. Cecchin, Lane, and Ray (1992) suggest that being in the knower position can be a trap for having to defend a position once it is taken. They take a position of irreverence about the position of knower, which they claim allows them to move in and out of different positions at various times and in various contexts. Their key premise is that "excessive loyalty to a specific idea makes the individual who embraces it irresponsible in relation to the moral consequences inherently involved" [p. 8]. They contend that if they believe in one set of ideas too adamantly they could lose the flexibility to question belief systems. When Cecchin et al. take a position of irreverence without acknowledging that there is also a place for reverence, do they not fall into the same trap they warn us about? Taking a position is a generic act. That act requires us to consider the position and its antithesis, or otherwise that position cannot be formulated. Bateson (1979) contended that taking a position about an idea requires a binocular view. His belief was that mind contains only the ability to recognize differences between ideas—for example, news of difference. Therefore, one idea—like irreverence—standing alone without its counterpart—reverence—cannot be useful to us in formulating our beliefs. From an ethical perspective, we must acknowledge both the legitimacy of knowing and not-knowing and of being both reverent and irreverent in different contexts and under various conditions as the dialogue demands. It is the same as our concern for invoking an I–It and I–Thou attitude in different contexts and under various conditions. Both are a part of any encounter with others.

One of the limits to our being in the knower position is about the views that clients provide about themselves and the meanings they give about their life experiences. Clients are the knowers of their own stories in spite of professional interpretations, diagnoses, and treatment plans. Hearing clients tell their own stories is more important than hearing about them from referring professionals. The stories are always richer in content and more personal and emotional than professional reports. Professional reports are clinical and usually devoid of compassion for their subjects. It is constraining to receive someone else's diagnosis, and it often colours therapists' experiences with families or closes the door on new information. This practice sets up competitive tensions between colleagues and clients. It would seem preferable to err on the side of not receiving information from others too soon. This means telling clients when we are not ready to see reports from hospitals or previous therapists, and telling referring therapists when we are not ready to hear their views. Learning about client's imaginings about their therapist's view of themselves is valuable. This process is a part of the ethical position we take. Clients are the primary source of information and are always listened to first.

This does not mean that the views of others are not legitimate. They are an acceptable part of the story we build with our clients. When they are put in the context in which they were formed, they become an important source of meaning-making for the psychotherapy. Our ethical position requires us to pay attention to those stories as they unfold in dialogue. In context, the stories of other professionals become an integral part of the meaning-making experience we have with the family. When we share with clients the meanings we are making of the stories they tell us, they incorporate our reflections into their stories as it makes sense to them. We do not believe that it is ethical to presume to re-author the stories of clients by promoting specific changes or solutions. Re-authoring another's story is to presume that one is the knower of what is in the best interests of the other. It is different from influencing another by communicating our understanding of the story. We feel that we can contribute our ideas to another person's story, which then influences both our story and the story of the other, without creating a hierarchy.

When observing the work of other family therapists, we find that children are most often treated as small adults. There is little emphasis given to creating a context in which children can tell their stories in their own language and with a feeling that they are being listened to and responded to as children. This may reflect a general attitude towards children in American society, analogous to the idiom that children should be seen and not heard. In some segments of American society, children sit low on the hierarchy of importance. It is our position relative to children that they must be given the same respect accorded adults. Often parents do not give children credit for seeing, hearing, and understanding much about the meanings of family dynamics. When children are allowed or encouraged to be part of the therapy, they are often a source of healing through understanding. Their insights and compassion can go far beyond their parents' imaginations. We are not comfortable in engaging in adult talk that leaves the children out. Consequently, we are forever checking in with children to make sure they are a part of the evolving conversation. Sometimes we take the risk of seeming to be disrespectful to the parents by asking for the opinions of the children (Inger & Inger, 1990b). We believe that everyone in the therapy session can expect equity, safety, and respect across generations and between genders. Women often have the same struggles as do the children in the family when fathers and sons dominate conversations. We are often impolite, but respectful, for the sake of opening a dialogic space for the females in the family.

In our attempt to create equity and safety in the therapy, we sometimes have to face the limitations of the work. There are times in the life of our clients when we cannot create enough safety or equity to justify the vulnerable position that therapy puts them in, such as when divorcing parents are at war and fighting is a higher priority than healing differences. It can mean either not beginning therapy or ending it before all that could be done is done. Under these uncertain circumstances, we find we must voice our concerns in a direct and respectful way.

THE CONTRIBUTION OF MARTIN BUBER TO AN ETHICALLY BASED THERAPY

We discovered that some of Martin Buber's thinking reminded us of what Gregory Bateson had been saying (see Inger & Inger, 1990a; Inger, 1993). Bateson had already had a profound influence on the thinking and practices of many family therapists, and some of his ideas were common knowledge in the family therapy field (Watzlawick, Jackson, & Beavin, 1967; Watzlawick, Weakland, & Fisch, 1974; Selvini-Palazzoli et al., 1978; Hoffman, 1981; Keeney, 1983; White, 1986; Andersen, 1987; Boscolo et al., 1987; Andersen, 1991). Both Buber and Bateson immersed themselves in experiences and then distanced themselves from those experiences in order to reflect and then make sense of them (Inger, 1993). Neither believed in the concept of objectivity. Both required immersion, distancing, reflection, and re-immersion in order to come up with the formulations of their experiences and their philosophies. They also demonstrated a respect for the points of view of others as legitimate in their own right. Buber (1965a) called this experience imagining the real or inclusion. Bateson (1972) considered it a "Learning III" phenomenon.

The wizened men also taught us that we must listen to ourselves as much as we listen to others and take both into account when we reach conclusions about experiences. The way we go through an experience, the things we attend to, say, and do, reflect and reveal our beliefs, epistemologies, and tautologies about how the world of the living and the non-living function. But it takes at least two somethings to make meaning and, thus, a relationship. For Buber (1958) it can be I–It or I–Thou, and for Bateson (1972, 1979) a binocular or multiple description of two or more of anything. For us, it means we have to consider multiple inputs from ourselves and others in order to understand meaning-making (Inger & Inger, 1990a, 1990b).

Buber (1965a) taught that intentions are important in a dialogue. If we approach a conversation with an attitude of I–It, we will have a different intention from how we approach it with an I–Thou attitude. An I–It attitude means one person regards the other as an object and will intend to use the relationship as a means to an end. An I–Thou attitude, on the other hand, connotes that one person enters the conversation with the intent to appreciate the other as a person and to value that person's otherness. The conversation is an end in its own right. The conversation itself is what is sought after when a person is in an I–Thou attitude (Shabatay, 1991, p. 138).

We discovered the importance of announcing our intentions in the therapeutic conversation when we feel it is safe. When we do not feel it is safe, we have also learned to announce our caution. This internal experience of intuiting through inclusion allows us to have a dialogue about the lack of safety in the therapeutic situation. Ethically, we believe that it is our obligation to keep our clients informed of our intentions and meaning-making. Keeping clients informed about our process allows us to request that they keep us informed about their process. When we are doing co-therapy, we speak with each other about our process, intentions, and the possible meanings of any changes that are taking place at any given moment.

Being with ourselves. Buber (1965a) informs us that if we strive for genuine dialogue we must first be able to be with ourselves.

> Certainly in order to be able to go out to the other you must have the starting place, you must have been, you must be, with yourself. [p. 21]

To be with ourselves is an internal experience of being present and receptive to our own internal voice. It means participating in internal commentary about what we are experiencing at the moment we experience it. This means being aware of our own thought patterns and feeling states as they come into awareness as we act and react to an experience. To be with ourselves also implies that, from time to time, we focus upon how we are reacting to a situation and how we are guiding ourselves through it. Remarking to ourselves about ourselves in relation to the situation is an aspect of being with ourselves. This experience of remarking to ourselves involves taking on a reflecting attitude about our experience as we focus on both the internal and external aspects of it. It means imagining multiple views of the experience. It also includes organizing our internal views relative to what we believe we are tracking about the external situation. This circular process—experiencing, reflecting, organizing, synthesizing, and re-experiencing—requires us to be vigilant about our contributions to the evolution of the situation.

In the dialogic encounter we can respond from an I–Thou or I–It attitude. So, too, do we respond to an encounter with ourselves within that framework. An internal I–It attitude is one in which we objectify ourselves. We hear ourselves in our own internal dialogue from an either/or or right/wrong perspective and are judgemental of one side of ourselves, thus choosing to close off ideas and feelings that do not coincide with judgements from the other side. Our internal attitude guides our dialogue with others. If we accept ourselves in our wholeness, value the diversity of our thinking and feeling, and appreciate the differences and uncertainties we encounter within ourselves, then we are experiencing the internal dialogue with an I–Thou attitude.

Bending towards others. Another basic step in developing a genuine dialogic attitude in therapy is the bending of oneself towards others as a way of attending to the experiences of others (Buber, 1965a, p. 22). As Buber put it, bending towards others is a way of

> . . . realizing the other in his particular existence, even the encompassing of him, so that the situations common to him and oneself are experienced from his, the other's end. [p. 23]

We discovered that was what we had been working towards for a long time, without a language for it. We were interested in our clients as they lived their lives. We wanted to know about them, how they lived, what they thought about their lives, not just what went wrong with the marriage, the kids, the jobs. We were interested in the depth of their experiencing and how they shared those experiences within the family and within their community. As social constructionists we were primarily interested in their constructions of meanings, their way of making sense of their experiences. We were forever veering away from the standard practice of ferreting out the symptoms, the deductive reasons for the symptoms, and the devising of clever ways to shoo the symptoms away and make things better or at least different. We were interested in the world views of our clients and their views of one another. We were interested in their concordant views as much as their discordant ones.

Taking this basic step of bending towards others means attending acutely to others in terms of how and what they are attempting to say. Simultaneously, the listeners must be aware of how they are receiving that which others are saying. In turning towards others, we have several ways we can receive what is being said to us. We can receive it positively with sympathy, compassion, empathy, or inclusion, or negatively as foreign, indifferent, irritating, or repulsive. Regardless of how we respond, it is important to be aware of how we received what is being said and what constraints it puts on us to have received it in that particular way. What we do with that awareness becomes the basis for how we use ourselves to respond. The next step in this sequence of perceiving ourselves in relation to others is to imagine how others might perceive our reaction to what they said. This recursive process of receiving what others say in its wholeness, then sensing what it means to us, and what our feedback might mean to others, provides the basic building blocks of an ethically based therapy. This can be an intense, complicated, and intricate way of being in relation to others in therapy. It requires that we suspend our judgemental tendencies long enough to immerse ourselves in an experience and to maximize the moment of encounter with another.

Therapists who work on bending towards others must be able to tolerate uncertainty and, thus, be vulnerable to the vagaries of the conversation that unfolds. We have to handle the vulnerability that often accompanies a commitment to being able to live with the uncertainty in dialogue. Holding on to the tension that uncertainty brings and using that tension is important for opening up the possibilities for the families to change (Inger & Inger, 1990a, 1990b). If we can tolerate and hold on to uncertainty, then sometimes the family can do the same thing. When therapists as well as families have difficulty tolerating the tensions of uncertainty, then new options get lost. Tolerating uncertainty and, thus, tolerating differences leads the way to honouring differences.

In order to honour differences, we must embrace the contraries we encounter in both what others tell us and in what we tell ourselves. Embracing the contraries is one way of making sense of the possibilities of dialogue. Tolerating differences and uncertainty is crucial in providing a safe-enough environment for a psychotherapeutic experience to take place.

Fully appreciating the differences and contraries encountered when talking to families occurs when therapists are able to immerse themselves in an encounter and to suspend judgement while not suspending thinking. Therapists have the opportunity to try on different ways of thinking and believing as the family talks. Immersion in dialogue creates a necessary condition for being able to take the position of others as we imagine others to be. Through this process of immersion, we can have an experience that does not require a final position to be taken, a judgement to be made, or an opinion or interpretation rendered. Inclusion (Buber, 1965a) allows therapists the opportunity to embrace contraries and yet not have to resolve them. The act of inclusion gives therapists an experience of sitting with or holding onto contradictions, conflicts in meaning, and seemingly incompatible dialogue. By immersing ourselves in conversation without the necessity of resolution, the opportunity is established for a compassionate dialogue.

Identifying the between. Buber (1965b) defines the *between* as that place,

> ... whose meaning is to be found neither in one of the two partners nor in both together, but only in their dialogue itself, in this "between" which they live together. [p. 75]

When people are in partnership in the realm of the *between* they fully appreciate each other's differences without losing sight of their own uniqueness. Genuine dialogue is the vehicle for the creation of the realm of the *between*. Even when one disagrees with the convictions of the other, one affirms the differences, struggles with these differences, and confirms the other as an opponent with genuine differences. The legitimization of differences reflects an ethical position of valuing differences and expecting that same attitude from the other in an atmosphere of safety and respect.

Any time that one person is in relationship to an other, he or she is also in a basic attitudinal relationship to him/herself. A person's self and the other are dialectically related, recursively bound, one to the other, as a primary perceptual and conceptual entity. There is no self without a relationship to the other, It or Thou. As pointed out earlier, Buber posited two basic movements that people make in relation to one another (1965a, p. 21), bending back to oneself (an orienting function) or turning towards the other (a realizing function). Bending back to oneself reflects an I–It attitude and represents a pragmatic orientation that objectifies the other. It lends itself to the construction of a self-contained individual, as described earlier. Turning towards the other reflects an I–Thou attitude and allows one to appreciate the other as the other from an aesthetic orientation. The act of turning towards the other constitutes the basic act of the ensembled individual who is in continuous relation with others, and boundaries between self and other are not tightly drawn. These two movements constitute two different ethical positions.

An ethically based family therapy emphasizes the realm of the *between* in addition to the internal process of each individual participant. Buber believed that trying to separate a conversation into discrete personal realities ignores the importance of the conversation as an unfolding of relationships in the present. Being present in the conversation is a way of confirming each other. Buber (1965b) contended that "the wish of every man to be confirmed as what he is, even as what he can become" [pp. 67ff] is essential to genuine conversation. Genuine conversation demands mutuality of confirmation. Confirmation is that interpersonal experience in which a person experiences another by imagining what that other is feeling, thinking, and knowing. In this imagining state, one does not give up one's own beliefs, feelings, thoughts, or knowing. Nor does one give up the distinctiveness of one's self. Rather, one imagines the other in his uniqueness, wholeness, and unity of being (Friedman, 1993). For therapists, the task is to be able to imagine the points of view of clients while simultaneously being aware of their own points of view. Holding two or more points of view simultaneously is one of the central tasks of therapists practising an ethically based perspective.

Figure 1 provides a visual context for thinking about an ethical position in relationship to clients. It is intended as a guide for the reader to the main concepts of an ethically based therapy as presented above. By following along with these phrases one can obtain an overall view of the flow of evolving an aesthetic sense of what an ethic of being constitutes, and then the reader can imagine how this can be applied in psychotherapy.

An ethic of care. Gilligan's (1982) idea of an ethic of care concerns the predominant values women are taught: namely, that relationships are primary and that women are essentially concerned with inclusiveness and shared experience. The different voice that women use seems more concerned with connections and fluidity of personal boundaries. This ethic contrasts with one presented earlier: the self-contained individual who is taught to be autonomous, disconnected, and separated by a clear personal boundary.

As Gilligan (1982) states,

> The ideal of care is thus an activity of relationship, of seeing and responding to need, taking care of the world by sustaining the web of connection so that no one is left alone. [p. 62]

This concept of an ethic of care resonates with Buber's concepts of mutuality, confirmation, and inclusion. Buber was dedicated to the idea that one person cannot exist alone or in isolation. One knows oneself only in relation to knowing another. Both participants, as Buber said, live "through the common event from the standpoint of the other" (1965a, p. 97). Living from the standpoint of the other connects Buber's concept of inclusion with Gilligan's concept of an ethic of care.

Gilligan's (1982) idea of "a web of connection" also had the familiar ring of Buber's "between"—the realm of the relationship itself, which is isomorphic to an ethic of care. Buber's comments about gender seem aptly applicable to Gilligan's ethic of care. Buber states,

> ... the genuinely thinking man must live through the feminine, the genuinely thinking woman the masculine; each must find

Being with ourselves

Using internal process as an orienting function

- Accepting the moment as real.
- Observing internal dialogue of thoughts, feelings, and reactions in the moment.
- Observing patterns of thoughts and feelings.
- Accepting the circularity of internal experiences.
- Holding the tensions of uncertainty.

Bending towards others

Using external process as a realizing function

- Attending to the external process.
- Accepting what is being said by the other.
- Attending from the perspective of the other (inclusion).
- Imagining how the other wants to be received.
- Being aware of the other's reception of the process.

Being in dialogue

Realizing the I–Thou relationship through dialogue

- Giving feedback based on a position of inclusion with others.
- Accepting feelings about the feedback.
- Being aware of the internal response to those feelings.
- Maintaining a process of bending towards the other.

Identifying and experiencing the between

- Immersing one's self in the moment of contact.
- Appreciating differences.
- Reconciling differences.
- Honouring the other as a genuine other.
- Experiencing the fluctuations and rhythm of moving in and out of I–Thou and I–It connections.
- Accepting the circularity of interactions.

Figure 1: Building Blocks of an Ethically Based Psychotherapy

therein the counterpole to his own in order to allow the unity of the spiritual life to develop from both. [cited in Friedman, 1991, p. 71]

Buber's ideal of living in dialogue resonates with Gilligan's (1982) idea that an ethic of care means living in a web of connection in which

> ... the vision that self and other will be treated as of equal worth, that despite differences in power, things will be fair; that vision that everyone will be responded to and included, that no one will be left alone or hurt. [p. 63]

Furthermore, the ethic of care is coincident with Buber's beliefs in the efficacy of community, the value of mutuality in relationships, and the importance of being in relationship with others in a way that validates the authenticity of oneself and others in their wholeness.

Gilligan's ethic of care and Buber's I–Thou relationship form for us a double description of what the process of relationships is about. Caring provides the affective and connective tone of the relationship experience, and an I–Thou attitude provides a way of going about the process of ensuring the mutuality of care. The juxtaposition of the two frameworks furthers the value of attachments in ongoing, life-long experiences within families and within the larger society. Embracing an ethic of care and an I–Thou attitude has allowed us to move away from those theories which propound an ethic of autonomy, separation, severation, hierarchy of relationships, and power and control. By introducing an ethic of care, we are able to work in a "both . . . and . . ." framework, seeing the value of each position relative to the context within which it is promoted and practised.

CHAPTER SIX

A consultation
with a therapist, a family,
and an audience

INTRODUCTION

"The eyes that fix you in a formulated phrase . . ."

T. S. Eliot, "The Love Song of J. Alfred Prufrock", 1936

We imagine clients must feel like J. Alfred Prufrock when we gaze at them, make judgements about them using our cool clinical ways of investigating them. Do they feel our fix on them and do they feel ". . . pinned and wriggling on the wall . . .", as did J. Alfred Prufrock? From our fix and gaze and interrogation of them, what is it they should presume about our intentions?

Therapists tend to hypothesize about individuals and families before they have met them. It is a part of the ritual of figuring out what we want to know and how we intend to go about finding out. It relieves feelings of uncertainty and powerlessness. It provides the illusion that we are knowers and doers and that we can figure out what is wrong with others and fix them. We hypothesize mostly about their lives outside the therapy interview and what has gone wrong that necessitates their having to come to us to change them. We do not attend to the experience they may be anticipating in the moment of the interview itself. We too often ignore what it is like for the family to be in the interview. We are more likely to focus on the content of the dilemmas or problems that brought them to the interview.

The following transcript is an illustration of how we applied an ethical perspective in an interview with a family and an audience of 75 therapists. In this interview, we focused on how the family was experiencing the process of the interview and what meanings they were deriving from that experience. We attended carefully to each family member's participation in order to ensure that they experienced safety in the conversation and that they were treated equitably. Since the interview took place at a workshop for mental health professionals, the audience and the family were in the same room. The family had agreed to be interviewed in this format as a way of obtaining a consultation that could help their son's therapist to help their son.

When the workshop began, we did not know the orientations of these 75 therapists. We knew we must be prepared to respond to their many viewpoints. We have often found that deeply held beliefs and ethical perspectives of professionals are expressed passionately when discussing specific family dynamics. Theoretical discussions are mild compared with the passion shown when talking about families who are thought to personify certain problems, symptoms, or constellations of behaviours. This experience was no exception.

The interview was divided into segments. First, we interviewed, Jon, the therapist, about his views of his client, Steve, and Steve's family. Second, we simulated an interview with the family using professionals from the audience. Next, we interviewed the family. Then, we discussed the interview with an observing team from the audience. The family came back for a brief conversation. Finally, we debriefed the entire experience with the observing team and the audience.

When reading the transcript of the interview with the family and the therapist, we ask the readers to be on the lookout for those moments in the dialogue which are representations of the ideas we have been discussing. Although we have annotated the interview and given you our ideas about what we were experiencing, we ask the readers to formulate their own opinion about these ideas— specifically, to be aware of those moments which represent demonstrations of such ethical constructs as being with ourselves, bending towards or away from others, moments of experiencing the between, and moments of demonstrating an ethic of care. We also ask the readers to take an overarching view of the interview and be aware of how patterns of the relationships develop among family members and between the family members and us.

PREPARING FOR THE INTERVIEW WITH THE FAMILY

The school had contracted with Jon for individual therapy for 12-year-old Steve. Jon had had no direct contact with the parents. Recently, the school had asked Jon to meet with Steve's parents, to evaluate them and to determine how they were contributing to Steve's difficulties in school. Being aware of the problem of the dual role he was being asked to play as individual and family therapist, and the school's assumption about the parents' culpability, Jon asked the family if they would be willing to come to the workshop and be interviewed by consultants. They consented.

It is often our practice to interview the therapist first and then to interview the family and the therapist together. As part of this process, our preconceived notions about the family come to the fore, and we often find ourselves in the uncomfortable position of forming alliances with colleagues to the disadvantage of the family whom we have not yet met. In spite of the best intentions of our colleagues, they and we have beliefs and prejudices about all sorts of things. We communicate these prejudices to one another without realizing the impact we are having on the development of the listeners' beliefs. We entered this experience realizing that we would be talking with the family after forming many ideas about them. When we are put in this position, our objective becomes one of trying to challenge our own preconceived ideas with open-minded and creative questions. After the interview, we can look at those preconceived notions and see how many we validated and, just as important, how many we invalidated.

* * *

The following is the transcript of our conversation with Jon and with the audience as we prepared for the interview. We have added annotations to give the readers insight into our thinking processes as the dialogue progresses.

We started by asking Jon to tell us what he knew about Steve and his family.

Jon: My client, Steve, is 12 years old. He has a younger brother Tim who is 10 years old. His mother's name is Rebecca, and his father's is Dan. Steve attends junior high school and has been labelled Severely Emotionally Disturbed. They call it S.E.D. The school asked me to see Steve in individual therapy and to find out what is going on at home that may be contributing to Steve's difficulties in school.

[The role we take in talking with the family comes with a presumption that we will find out what is going on at home, and sounds somewhat like detective work. This could possibly be construed by the family as adversarial. We question whether this is an appropriate role for us relative to the family. From the beginning we believe we are in an ethical dilemma, but not an unusual one. This is a typical situation in which someone or some agency seeks confirmation for its views from other professionals.]

Jon: Steve is described by the teachers and the staff in the S.E.D. program as a very strange young boy. He is withdrawn, appears dishevelled, and confused. He's very, very, bright. I've had four or five sessions with him. At the second session he talked about a behaviour loop that he goes through. He told me that he becomes anxious and gets really tense. Then he has a horrible fight with his parents, things calm down and get better, and then he gets anxious again and has a horrible fight with his parents. He seems to be able to talk to adults with some facility, but he has a lot of trouble in his peer relationships. He's probably the most picked-on kid at the junior high school. He's also failing a lot of his classes. The school people think it is because of his emotional disturbance.

[Now we have a vivid description of how others see this child. What do we do with such a description? To accept it is to constrain us from having our own experience of this boy and his family. To reject it is possibly to miss some important things about him from the point of view of some of the people with whom he is coming into contact at school. Thus, we must keep a "both . . . and . . ." perspective about the boy in relation to the others who have assigned certain attributes to him. They believe he is emotionally disturbed—an attribution that carries a good deal of seriousness with it. We usually try to suspend our beliefs long enough to have an experience with others, like Steve, especially others who have already made a great impact on the people who are judging them.]

Ivan: What do they mean by emotional disturbance?

Jon: It means that he's in the upper two percent of kids in the school whose emotional disturbances are interfering with their work.

Ivan: So, once he's in a percentage you can identify it?

Jon: Right. If he was in the upper three percent then it wouldn't be enough, and he wouldn't be S.E.D.

[Both Ivan and Jon respond facetiously to the idea that percentage has become a criterion for emotional disturbance.]

Ivan: So, there's a very fine distinction between two and three percent?

[At this very early part of the process, Ivan has thrown himself into an internal state of being with his own dilemma about the way this boy has been labelled. He is struggling to overcome both his prejudice about the label and the prejudice the label represents. It demands of Ivan that he allow himself to let this simmer and hold the tension reflected by his comments. It is a good example of living with concepts that are difficult to believe.]

Jon: Right.

Ivan: And do they line the children up everyday to determine this percentage? (Group laughter.)

[Ivan finds himself needing to shake off the constraints of this idea of categorizing this boy and putting him in a percentage of an abstract population of children who are presumed to share characteristics that justify this category in the first place. Humour helps us find new perspectives. Humour is a way of trying on a distancing experience when the bending towards an idea or a person seems too overwhelming at the moment.]

Audience Member: He has to have interferences in two out of three areas: family, social, and school in order to qualify.

[In spite of our apparent difficulty, this person tries to bring us back to the particular reality that the school has constructed for us. It all sounds scientific and orderly, percentages and something called "interferences". These are official-sounding ideas. They put certainty into conversations where we would otherwise feel uncertain.]

Ivan: So, the important part of this is that the school considers him very seriously disturbed, not by attributes of any internal process, but by social and educational standards. What does the school tell you about their concerns? What does he do to worry them?

Jon: He is immature. He makes a lot of funny noises in class. Inappropriate noises. He has long conversations that sort of trail off to nowhere. He will start to answer the question that the teacher asks and then change the subject four or five times in a couple of minutes. It is very confusing for all the students who are trying to listen to him, and most confusing for the teachers.

Ivan: In your context with him, have you had that experience?

[We are often curious about how differently people behave in different contexts. It helps us to clarify what may be happening in the particular context that seems to trigger off specific behaviours. Is Jon put off by Steve? Is Jon moving towards or bending away from Steve? Questions are going through our minds about whether Steve is being experienced by Jon in an I–It or I–Thou context.]

Jon: He's very difficult to keep on track. We have spent some time talking about how difficult it is for him to stay on track. In our last session, he was still having a lot of difficulty staying on track. He apologized for it. He said: "I know I'm not on track. I'll get back to it."

Jeri: So he's developed some ability to reflect on his own behaviour?

[Having the ability to reflect on our behaviour often signifies a certain level of discomfort with it as well as a readiness to change it.]

Jon: Yes, exactly. He's a very affable, very friendly kid.

Jeri: And is he that way in school, too?

[Jeri's idea about Steve's reflectivity is confirmed, and now she tries to look for it in different contexts.]

Jon: The teacher in the S.E.D. classroom said he just starts talking and continues until people get irritated with him. When they get irritated, he insults someone in the class and then gets punched.

Jeri: Do the parents report this same thing too? Is that part of the anxiety, fight, anxiety, fight cycle?

Jon: Yes, the parents report that he can be very irritating at times. His younger brother, Tim, is very angry with him all the time.

Jeri: This is a single marriage of an intact family? Are there any complications?

Jon: None, except that they're in the process of adopting a five-year-old girl from Colombia.

Jeri: When did they start that process?

Jon: I don't know when they started the process. They were supposed to go to Colombia in January to pick up the little girl, but it got postponed, so they're going in March.

Jeri: Do you think that has any relationship to Steve's behaviour now?

[At this point, Jeri looks for the possibility of linkages of meaning to the behaviours Steve is described as exhibiting.]

Jon: No, I don't think so. Steve has been seeing counsellors and school psychologists since he was six years old for pretty much the same problem.

Ivan: Has anybody evaluated Steve for differences in his learning style?

[Again, Ivan tries to take a negative attribute and see if it is merely a difference and can be reframed.]

Jon: I don't think they have done that. They have done some school psychology evaluations to figure out what he does well and what he doesn't do well, but they haven't really evaluated his style of learning. They say he should be getting good grades, he's very intelligent, and they don't know what's going on.

Ivan: That's what some people might consider an important error. The idea that there is one kind of intelligence, and it is independent of learning styles. They can't figure him out, so they put him in the S.E.D. classroom?

Jon: Right. And he's unhappy. Since he's unhappy, the school concludes there must be something wrong with him.

Jeri: So, we have a larger system in the room with us that we're trying to understand, and to relate to. If it wasn't this school, it would be some other larger system probably, since we're all interconnected with larger systems. Jon, what is your relationship with the larger system and the family?

[Jeri wants to know what constraints Jon experiences in his relationship with Steve. Is it at all possible for Jon to experience Steve in his own right, or is his experience seriously influenced by the nature of his relationship with the larger system and the family? Is Jon aware of those constraints? We will be interested to what extent it might be possible for Jon to enter a genuine dialogic experience with Steve and not objectify him.]

Jon: My role at the school is, well . . . I'm not exactly sure, in this context. I work with Steve in individual counselling, but the school wants me to provide them with some information about the family. And they want me to give them some ideas of how best to work with Steve in the classroom so that he can be more successful.

Ivan: And the family knows this?

Jon: Right. I told them I wanted to meet with them together with Steve so that I could get some more information that would be helpful to the school and to Steve without breaking confidentiality with Steve.

[We have here an interesting issue. We have the confidentiality of Steve to protect, but not that of the parents. Why are the parents not afforded this same protection? Does it represent a duality of values? Is it an example of the bias towards the individual and not the collective? We note this duality for possible later reference.]

Ivan: And this is your meeting?

Jon: Right.

Audience Member: What are Steve's perceptions of his parents?

Jon: He is very protective of his parents and is always telling me that things are getting better. In the past there was a lot of conflict between Steve and his mother. He was particularly aware of his anger at her. There is also a lot of anger between Steve and his father, although his father works a lot so he isn't around very much.

[This could be a warning of how Steve will interact with his parents. Our task is to take in this information but not be married to it; that is, not to try to confirm or deny it. To do so would be to invite Steve to act out our belief about who he is, yet we have to hold this information.]

Ivan: What does his father do?

Jon: His father works for a tyre company. Steve has moved a lot throughout his school years because they've been moved around by the company.

Ivan: Does it mean Father changes tyres, or is he a salesman?

Jon: He's in a middle-management position.

Ivan: Does the mother work outside the home?

Jon: No. Rebecca is at home full-time.

Ivan: So there is conflict between Steve and Rebecca. Do we know what the conflict is?

Jon: Mom says that Steve has always been a different child. He has always been extremely quiet and withdrawn, and she has felt a kind of gulf between them. She has been very uncomfortable with it.

Jeri: She sees him as withdrawn. Does he see her as needing protection?

[Jeri introduces what seems to be contradictory ideas for us to think about. As much as possible we try to open our thoughts to a multitude of possibilities which define and describe behaviours. In this case, Jeri is opening the door to the possibilities of the recursive aspects of their relationship as opposed to thinking about behaviours as static, unconnected.]

Jon: I'm not sure if he sees her that way, or if he sees the system as kind of dangerous. "You don't want to say too many things about your family to the system because the system can get you."

Jeri: And aren't you a part of that system?

Jon: Sure.

[We have at this point established that Jon has a dual relationship with Steve. He tries to assure Steve that he has his best interests in mind, but at the same time he works for the school system. This could be the classical dilemma many therapists find themselves in, serving two clients with possible differences in their interests.]

Audience Member: You are like an investigator.

Jon: Yes, I could find out some horrible stuff. He apparently told Mom that he couldn't tell me the truth because she might get put in jail. And she has no idea what he's talking about.

Jeri: Did she tell you that?

Jon: She did.

Audience Member: Has Steve mentioned criminal activity?

Jon: Not that I know of.

Jeri: I wonder if that was a metaphor. Perhaps he feels some form of neglect or abuse.

[This idea about what Steve could tell about the mother is obviously a very attractive piece of information. For a detective it could lead to solving a crime. For some therapists it could lead to the objectification of the mother and Steve and define an entire interview. For us, it represents a danger signal that could close off dialogue and could constrain us from entering the conversation with them from the standpoint of caring about how we help construct this interview. We now know we must be cautious.]

Jon: Or that somehow his mother is not very good at mothering?

Audience Member: What's Tim like?

Jon: I know very little about Tim except that he is angry at Steve. And he is more outgoing, more successful at school, and has more friends.

Audience Member: What's the relationship like between Tim and Mom?

Jon: Mom describes it as closer. My impression from what she said was that it was more satisfying for her. Tim is more responsive as a son.

Jeri: What is Steve's relationship with his Dad like?

Jon: It's not much of a relationship. His Dad works a lot and is not around. I got reports that he occasionally gets mad at Steve and yells.

Ivan: Yells. No hitting? Does Mom hit?

Jon: Not that Steve has reported.

Ivan: Is there any love in the family? Do they love each other? Do they have a language for loving, for being affectionate?

[As a matter of principle, we ask about the complement of an action, belief, thought, or feeling in order to see if there is a possible recursive relationship. This helps us not become locked into our ideas too soon. It is based on the principle of binocular vision as a way of establishing that every idea has its antithesis. And it is important to acknowledge both. When we think about a broad range of ideas we can ask about them and listen to the answers.]

Jon: Mom talks a lot about loving, loving her kids, and hoping to
provide a loving environment. She talks a lot about wanting to be
able to communicate, encouraging her kids to communicate.

*[Jon's response tells us there is some depth to the mother's interest in her
children. Had we only focused on anger and other negatives we might have
missed out on the possibility that the family has a range of feelings and
relationships that reflect their feelings.]*

Jeri: Ivan, you have brought in the concept of love for some reason?
Are you beginning to hypothesize about the family? What we
must remember is that hypothesizing will most likely tell us
more about ourselves than about the family. What about hypothesizing? Any ideas?

*[Jeri's comment was designed to encourage further inquiry about the posi-
tives in the family. However, as we shall see, when she invited hypotheses,
negative hypotheses began to pour in.]*

Audience Member: What about the idea that Steve is distracting
the family from conflict between Mom and Dad?

*[This is the classical triangulation we have all come to believe in as family
therapists. This idea reflects the triangle of the child who will sometimes
sacrifice himself for the good of his parents.]*

Audience Member: Steve's increased activity and S.E.D. label
might serve to make it more difficult for the family to keep
moving and force them somehow to slow down.

Audience Member: Or the opposite: if they keep moving, he
doesn't have to form relationships.

Ivan: Yes, that's the point of a hypothesis. Once you have one you
have to develop its complement as a possibility, otherwise you
get stuck in one-sided thinking.

Audience Member: Oh. So the opposite of the first hypothesis
could also be that, rather than being a distraction, he may make
them look at the situation. Pay attention.

Audience Member: Or he's trying to get some attention because
they're so involved with each other.

Audience Member: Or his behaviour might force Mother and Father to come together to address him.

Ivan: A generic hypothesis might be that Steve has been different from birth, and that the family has learned to respond to him in any number of ways. Sometimes a noticeable difference in a person can organize the meaning system rather than suggesting the meaning system is to blame for a problem being created. The meaning system then organizes around the reactions to these differences in trying to incorporate and make sense of them.

Jeri: Trustworthiness is an extremely important issue. Important because we never know what we are about to encounter. For example, Steve's comment to his mother about going to jail if he told the real truth could mean we would have a dilemma on our hands.

[We want the audience to know that through the hypothesizing they become a part of the contact we will have with the family. And just as we are hypothesizing about the family, the family is coming with many expectations about us, one of which may be about our trustworthiness. We may be perceived as part of the school system, which they may or may not trust.]

Ivan: So, we must look for intentions. Not just the family's intentions but the larger systems intentions, and our own intentions in this context. How are the family's intentions interpreted by the school, and how are the school's intentions interpreted by the family? It is important to talk about that difference before we get into any of these depthful dynamics.

[At this point we are introducing an important ethical principle that will guide our interactions. Our intentions are as much under scrutiny as are those of the family. We always question ourselves about our intentions, motives, and purposes. We have to have an internal dialogue that involves acknowledging our own participation in the conversation with the family.]

Audience Member: What was their response when you asked them to come here?

Jon: Mom was quite eager. She said Dad would have to get some time off work, but he will be here.

Ivan: And what did you tell them they were coming for?

Jon: They were coming for a consultation that would be helpful for me in my work with Steve and any future work with the family. I also told them this was going to be a training workshop and there would be an audience.

Jeri: We find that it is not unusual for families who really want help to be willing to come and sit in an arena like this in order to get special help and attention.

* * *

As we finished talking to the therapist and the audience about the family, we had the impression that specific expectations about what Steve and his parents were like had already been formulated. The fact that he was labelled S.E.D made sense to many in the audience who worked with the school systems. This label seemed to conjure up many images about what this child would be like and what his parents must be like.

After this discussion we had the audience simulate the family we were about to interview. Out of the simulation came even more negative fantasies of what these family members were going to be like. The parents were portrayed in a very negative light as neglectful, out of touch, *laissez-faire*, emotionally distant, and unavailable, and the boy was portrayed as withdrawn, non-communicative, and sullen. The family was simulated as being out of control, neither cohesive nor coherent as a family. We believed that the audience had readied themselves for seeing a very difficult, dysfunctional family who would be uncooperative, mistrustful, and wary of our motives. We also felt caught in the middle in the simulation, between audience and family and between family and school. It was not atypical of our experience as therapists and consultants to be in the middle of conflicts of interest between families and the social and economic systems with which they interface.

What was the ethical position to take in such a circumstance? How could we talk to the family and not be overly influenced by what we had experienced in this simulation? Our task was to find a way to be equitable to the family in the context of predetermined attributes as well as equitable to the audience who had, in good faith, revealed their fantasies and beliefs about the people we were about to encounter. How could we talk to the family so we could be trustworthy to them at the same time we were trying to be trustworthy to the audience, to the school, and to the therapist? This was the dilemma we carried to the interview with the therapist and the family.

THE INTERVIEW
WITH THE FAMILY AND THE THERAPIST

Ivan: [Indicating to the audience] We have met everybody out in the corridor. You are Rebecca, Dan, Steve, and Tim.

[Rebecca and Dan are the parents, Steve is the oldest son, and Tim is the youngest son. The family took seats facing away from the audience. Rebecca sat on the far left, next to her was Dan, then Tim, then Steve, and Jon was on the far right. Ivan and Jeri sat facing them, Jeri closest to Rebecca and Ivan closest to Jon.]

Jeri: Some of us are a little nervous.

[In the hallway prior to the interview, Rebecca had volunteered to Jeri that she was nervous. In exchange, Jeri acknowledged that she too was nervous. We try to let the family know what we are experiencing as we keep them posted about our experience with them.]

Ivan: I also told the family that these are nice people [referring to the audience with a gesture]. I wanted them [the family] to know that.

[This is our way of trying to reassure the family in a potentially anxiety-producing context.]

Jeri: We want you to know that the therapists in the audience are watching us and our work. We appreciate your being here to help them do that.

Ivan: Jon, you could help by telling us about your work with Steve up to now. Tell us your idea of how we might be useful to you and the family today.

[This is part of our consultation model. We are there to help the therapist.]

Jon: Steve and I are working together at the junior high where Steve is a student. We talk a lot about what goes on in class, about his classmates, things like that. When I first started working with Steve, I talked to Rebecca on the phone. I said that at some point I would like to get together with the family to learn some things about them that could help me in my work with Steve.

Ivan: [To Steve] Is it okay for Jon to say these things?

Steve: Yeah.

[Early in an interview we usually check in with the person identified as the client, especially when someone talks about him or her. We attempt to provide safety for the identified client so that he or she does not feel alienated. We hope to prevent the identified client from being overexposed and vulnerable before a safe-enough context has been created. In addition, we pay special attention to how children feel in this context. We want to let them know that we intend to make it safe for them to speak.]

Ivan: [To Jon] How do you think he is doing with what you are saying?

[By checking with the therapist, Ivan tries to make sure that Steve is not just answering out of politeness or shyness. This is a way of letting Steve know how serious we are about maintaining his emotional safety and looking for genuine answers.]

Jon: My guess is, if it makes him real uncomfortable, he'll say something.

Ivan: Okay.

Jon: But, if it only makes him a little uncomfortable, he might not say anything.

Ivan: So we might not know? [To Steve] Would it be all right with you if Jon helped us? Perhaps if he sees something making you a little uncomfortable he could tell us?

[By creating an atmosphere of safety, trust, and respect, we are attending

to the beginning process of creating a "between". By slowing down the conversation, we make it clear that the process is our main concern. We are not in a hurry to get into the content of the conversation if it jeopardizes the process of forming relationships. For us, it is more important how we proceed than what we proceed about.]

Steve: Yeah.

Ivan: That's okay?

Steve: Mmmm.

[We want Steve to know to what great lengths we will go to maintain safety for him, if necessary.]

Jeri: It occurs to me that as you ask Steve how we will know when he is uncomfortable that, as you look at him, Rebecca, you will know if he is uncomfortable.

Rebecca: He's real uncomfortable right now.

Jeri: Really?

Rebecca: Definitely.

[Jeri's belief about Rebecca is based on earlier exchanges of feelings. Rebecca showed signs of sensitivity, reflectivity, and honesty. Jeri will attempt to encourage Rebecca to give voice to these characteristics. Also, Jeri has established that it is legitimate for the mother to intervene on behalf of her son. This is an indication that we respect the family's dynamics.]

Ivan: Does that make you more uncomfortable, Rebecca?

Rebecca: No, not really. I feel fine, as long as you don't ask me anything [laughs].

[Rebecca is letting us know that she can allow Steve to be uncomfortable without becoming more uncomfortable herself. This allows her to differentiate her own discomfort from that of her son.]

Ivan: [To Rebecca] What about Dan? Do you think he's uncomfortable too, or is he doing all right?

Dan: I'm okay.

[We assume Dan can speak for himself, but we are interested to know whether Rebecca is as sensitive to her husband's feelings as she is to her son's feelings. Dan speaks for himself, and what we learn is that the parents can differentiate their individual needs from that of the other.]

Jeri: [To Steve] Boy, your Mom sure does know. How does she know, Tim?

[We are interested in Tim's perception of his mother's reflectivity and sensitivity. Furthermore, Jeri has now completed the circle of involving all the family in this conversation.]

Tim: She knows 'cause she has had more experience.

Jeri: I thought maybe it was the way he kicked his foot just now. [To Tim] Was it the foot that told her? No. Okay.

[Jeri uses this opportunity to bring Tim into the conversation while using humour. He, too, shows the ability to reflect and differentiate in spite of the anxiety aroused by the content of this conversation.]

Rebecca: I know that when they are comfortable they do more talking.

Ivan: Oh, so these are guys who talk when they're comfortable.

[Ivan is differentiating these guys from others who talk when they are uncomfortable. This is often a helpful distinction for therapists and family members.]

Rebecca: Oh yeah, definitely.

Jeri: Let's get back to Jon.

Jon: I'm glad to have the opportunity to have the family together. It will enhance my work with Steve.

Ivan: [To Jon] So this would be for you?

Jon: Yes, this is primarily for me.

[By bringing Jon in, Jeri eases the discomfort shown by the family and lets us again show concern for their safety.]

Ivan: [To Jon] What do you think you need to know that would be helpful in your work with the family? What might you want to know from them that would relate to your work with Steve?

Jon: Well, I'd like to know what Steve is like at home. What kind of things are going on in the family. What they've tried to do to make things more pleasant. Things like that.

Ivan: Would that make them more nervous or less nervous?

Jon: Probably more nervous.

Ivan: Yes, because I was thinking . . . [watching Rebecca move uneasily in her chair] that we don't want to move too fast.

[Ivan is concerned that he has made a mistake by asking Jon a question that might be too much for this rather shy family at this point in the interview. It might be an objectifying question and one that will inhibit genuine contact.]

Rebecca: I'll let you know.

Ivan: All right.

[We are setting the stage for the therapist to learn more about the family and how they relate to one another. These questions slow down the process and provide family members opportunities to reflect silently, to ask questions of us and each other, and to respond to us and each other, allowing their emotions to catch up with the verbiage. The overall effect of this is to create safety in the session. The secondary gain is that people eventually learn how do this outside the therapy context and, thereby, bring more safety into their dialogues elsewhere.]

Jeri: Tim, what makes you less nervous?

Tim: I don't know.

Jeri: Okay. Does Dad know when you're nervous as well as Mom does?

Tim: No. He's never around.

Ivan: What does he do?

Tim: He works on tyres. Now he's starting to get home when I get home from school. So we have more time.

Ivan: Really? What's changed?

Tim: My Dad always has to do the shift. He goes to work really early and comes back really late. In January he did a long shift, so now he comes home early.

Ivan: Really?

Jeri: So, he had his long shift in January, and now he's home after school?

Tim: Yeah.

Jeri: And how is that for you?

Tim: That's a lot better. We are building an addition to our house, and we're working together.

Jeri: You're working together with your Dad?

Tim: Yeah.

Jeri: Are you hammering? Or are you giving him the nails?

Tim: Well, we're starting to paint now.

Jeri: You are starting to paint. You're well along!

[It is our belief that we will get to know a family in the way that they introduce themselves. As we immerse ourselves in their interests, we can begin the process of inclusion. That is, we can come to know them from their points of view, their meanings, and their preoccupations. We are in no hurry to be clinical about this interview. Our objective is to be in conversation with them about them and about what is important to them. Any other agenda we have must be secondary.]

Ivan: Wow! You guys move fast. You just started in January [it is now mid-February].

Tim: Oh well, we have been building it for a long time.

Jeri: Is he a good partner?

Tim: Yep.

[We are hearing from Tim that things in the family are changing. Jon had told us that Father was never home. Tim tells how that has changed. This is why it is important not to act prematurely on hypotheses or to let our assumptions become concretized as if they are facts. Families and their circumstances change as time moves along. We must remain fluid in our thinking.]

Ivan: Where's Mom when you're doing this building?

Tim: Making snacks and stuff.

Ivan: So she has her job.

Tim: Yeah.

Jeri: And Steve, where's he?

Tim: He's either watching TV or playing with the computer.

Jeri: Computer. Hmmm. [To Steve] What do you play on the computer?

Steve: Well, I have different games. I have mysteries and problem-solving things or . . . I usually am watching TV more than I am playing the computer now.

Jeri: So, hammering and painting are not your thing?

[Jeri gingerly approaches Steve's relationship with his father because Jon warned that their relationship was distant. We started to realize that Jon's information about the family came from information received from teachers. Jon did not have first-hand knowledge of the parents.]

Steve: I'm not very good with my hands . . .

Jeri: Really, you look pretty good.

Ivan: So how do you work the computer?

Steve: Well, sometimes I'll just . . .

[We are trying humour again. We will continue to use humour throughout the session in hopes that they will begin to see themselves in a reflective light.]

Jeri: [To Ivan] You mean you want to know if he uses his hands?

[This is the first of many examples of how a co-therapy process works. This is a clarifying gesture Jeri makes towards Ivan and Steve. It is the responsibility of each member of the co-therapy team to be aware of those times when one of them is not being clear.]

Ivan: Yeah.

Jeri: He wants to know if you use your hands on the computer?

Steve: Yeah.

Ivan: Don't you have to do this [making hand motions as if typing on a keyboard]? Are you a pretty good typist?

Steve: Yeah.

Ivan: But not a good hammerer?

Steve: No.

[This is our first indication of Steve's self-effacing attitude. Yet, we do not highlight such an observation. We hold it because our interest lies in the flow of this conversation. We are interested in where all this will take us. We are not interested in redirecting for our own interests or purposes.]

Rebecca: He's being really hard on himself because he's been out there. He has hammered. He's been helping when we put down the floor.

Steve: That was a while ago.

Ivan: Why do you think he is being so hard on himself?

[We ask family members for their hypotheses as a way of building a family's story together. Everyone's input is sought. It is usually more productive to follow the leads of the clients than to try to direct the content of the conversation. By following their flow, we are better able to have an inclusive experience with them which leads to an experience in the between—that place where the dialogue has a life of its own and the meanings are evolved by all.]

Rebecca: That's a good question. He's very, very hard on himself.

Steve: I don't really know that I am.

Ivan: Your Mom says you've always been hard on yourself. Can you think of a time you've been easy on yourself?

[Ivan risks challenging Steve, albeit delicately, and Ivan is ready to back away at any moment.]

Steve: I'm sure there's probably been a lot of times, but I don't know. I'm not really sure.

Rebecca: A lot of times he won't try.

Jeri: Rebecca, can you think of a time when he has been easy on himself?

Rebecca: Hmmm. Easy on himself . . . [Long silence] Nope [softly].

Ivan: It must be very important for him to be hard on himself.

[When a family member introduces an idea about how another member is (e.g. what attribution they attach to that person), we introduce its complement. In this case the complement of "hard on yourself" is "easy on yourself". In this way we can have a conversation about the recursive nature of the positive and negative attribute and introduce ideas of the relative value of an attribute.]

Rebecca: Either that or he just hasn't ever gotten out of that mind set.

Jeri: [To Ivan] He never got out of that mind set. What do you think that means about how he got into that mind set? Do you think it has to do with anybody else in the family?

[Jeri is introducing two ideas. First, the idea of whether or not he can control his attitude, and second, whether his attitude might be shared within the family. This is the beginning of a process of sorting out complementary and symmetrical characteristics.]

Ivan: He might have backed into it. Sometimes people back into things without knowing it, and they just keep on doing it.

Jeri: You mean they don't know where they're headed, but then they get stuck? Anybody else in the family hard on themselves?

[Jeri comes in to help Ivan clarify his meaning and to broaden the question into a potentially confirmatory experience of shared beliefs in the family. This is a common practice in a co-therapy context, to help clarify a meaning by means of double description. We talk about the options of how one gets stuck in a mind set. This gives Rebecca time to think about her point of view without having to answer questions and declare herself. At the same time, the question has now been raised about whether this is a shared attribute rather than an isolated or unique characteristic carried by only one member of the family.]

Rebecca: Dan is.

Dan: Yeah, I am. I'm hard on myself.

Ivan: Did you back into it also, or did you make a decision to be hard on yourself?

[By using the family's phrase of "being hard on yourself", Ivan lets the family know that we are listening to how they use words and that we are attempting to understand their meanings. This is a step towards the experience of inclusion. The conversation is turning into one about how the family experience themselves rather than how outsiders like teachers and therapists judge them.]

Dan: I think it's a combination of both. Sometimes I find myself deciding to be hard on myself, and sometimes I find myself having it approach me, and I kind of realize that I'm in that situation. And sometimes there are different reactions. You can step back and think, gosh, I really need to lighten up here. Did that really count that much? Other times, you know . . .

Jeri: You actually think that way?

[Jeri disrupts Dan in genuine amazement. Dan has just told us about his ability to reflect upon his actions. In light of the information we were given about this father, we are truly amazed and impressed with his reflectivity, sensitivity, and ability to articulate both. Now we must let go of our stereotypic misconception of this man and his family. Our misconceptions could interfere with our ability to hear them in their own right. If we continue to invoke misperceptions, we will have a mis-meeting.]

Dan: Yeah . . .

Jeri: You can back away and observe it?

Dan: Sometimes. [Laughs] Sometimes.

Jeri: That's very impressive.

Dan: It's easier to do it the decision way than . . .

Ivan: You mean sometimes you decide, "I'm going to be hard on myself"?

Dan: Yeah, sometimes when you feel your performance demands that you be hard on yourself, then you decide to be hard on yourself.

Ivan: Do you think Steve knows how to do that? [To Steve] Do you know how to do what your Dad just said he knows how to do? To step back, to say: "Why am I doing this?" And he makes a decision whether to be hard on himself or not?

Steve: No. I don't really know how to do that.

[Ivan is looking to see if this is a shared attribute between father and son, furthering the question about shared attributes. It is also a question about Steve's ability to see his connectedness to his father.]

Jeri: How do you think your Dad learned how to do that?

Steve: Well he probably got . . . well he probably . . . probably just learned from, you know, what he was going through. He probably just learned from getting himself knocked down a few times.

Ivan: Really? He had some hard knocks?

Steve: I don't know, but probably.

Ivan: [To Steve] Have you had some?

Steve: Yeah.

[Ivan has made a calculated guess that since Steve was faltering, he was probably thinking about himself.]

Ivan: Have you been knocked down?

Steve: Mmm-huh [Yes].

Ivan: Did you learn the same way he has learned?

Steve: I don't learn very much.

Ivan: You don't? You mean you're already set in the way you do things?

Steve: No, I don't learn very quickly but, . . .

Ivan: So you're careful about learning?

Steve: [Sigh] Yeah.

[Steve says he does not learn very much, and he is a slow learner. Ivan introduces a positive alternative by suggesting that he is a careful learner. This offers Steve options to think about.]

Rebecca: He approaches people very cautiously. 'Cause people tend to hurt him. He interprets, or it seems to me, he interprets a lot of actions in a different way than other people.

Ivan: Tim, did your Mom say something that upset you?

[Ivan abruptly turns to Tim out of concern for his non-verbal reaction at that moment.]

Tim: No. It's just that it seems my brother knows a lot, but he just wants to get bad grades. I don't know why, but he just likes to get bad grades.

Ivan: Why do you think a guy would like to get bad grades?

Tim: To get attention.

Jeri: Wait! I've got to go slow because this is amazing. You think that he knows a lot, but he just gets bad grades in order to get attention?

[Jeri is amazed that Tim is aware of how smart Steve is, and that Tim has given so much thought to this dilemma that he has come up with his own hypothesis.]

Tim: Well, it's just that I know he's really smart, and . . .

Ivan: He's really smart?

Tim: Yeah.

Ivan: Does he know that?

Tim: Yes!

Jeri: Wow!

Ivan: He knows that.

Steve: I'm definitely top of the class!

[What a different response compared with Steve's previous self-effacing remarks. Tim has inadvertently brought out a side of Steve that is positive, self-confident, and may never have been seen in the school system.]

Ivan: You're definitely top?

Steve: Yeah. I should be.

Tim:. I think everybody makes fun of him because he's so smart.

[Tim offers us his very valuable hypothesis about why his brother is treated badly at school by his peers.]

Ivan: Really? He's so smart that they make fun of him.

Steve: I think I should be in a higher grade, but I'm just not motivated, 'cause, I mean, I've gone through review like this for the past four years. School's boring, you don't learn almost anything.

[This is Steve's hypothesis about why he does not produce in school. He believes he is bored and confined to reviewing subjects he already knows.]

Ivan: Is that right? But they haven't caught onto this yet at school?

Steve: I've tried to tell people.

Ivan: Who have you tried to tell?

Steve: I don't know. I've told my Mom and Dad. Actually they're the ones who got the idea.

[The hypothesis is a shared view with his parents. It is also a view known to Tim. They must talk about all this at home.]

Ivan: So who did they tell?

Steve: I don't know.

Jeri: If Dad is similar to you by being hard on himself, is he also similar to you in being very, very smart?

Steve: Um-huh. [Yes]

Ivan: So he's smart too?

Jeri: Does anyone know that Dad is smart?

Ivan: [To Tim] You must be smart, because you're the one who brought this whole thing up.

Jeri: Do people know that Dad is smart?

Tim: [Whispers] I'm smart too.

Jeri: [Also responding to Tim] You are too!

Ivan: You must have two smart parents because I think smart kids come from smart parents.

Rebecca: No.

Ivan: No?

Rebecca: No, I just come along for the ride.

Ivan: Wait a minute!

Jeri: Sounds like one more person is hard on themselves.

[We now get a glimpse of the possible origin of Steve's self-effacing attitude.]

Ivan: Yes. Not only that, but, that's where we started the conversation that Steve doesn't think a lot of himself. We now have a dilemma here.

[It is important that we have picked up on that earlier comment about people being hard on themselves. It turns out that being hard on oneself is part of a basic attitude held by the family. It is becoming clear to us that this whole family believes that being hard on oneself is an important attribution.]

Jeri: Yes.

Ivan: So we have a family that's hard on itself, but smart. [To Rebecca] Except, you won't accept being smart?

Rebecca: Well, I'm smart, but I'm not like him [Steve] or this one [Tim], or this one [Dad], in the sense that, you know, I'm bored.

Jeri: You're also the only woman in the family.

[Jeri surfaces the idea of gender and the possible negative effects gender politics has on how Rebecca sees herself in relation to the males in the family.]

Rebecca: Yes, that's right. So far.

Jeri: Does that make a difference? So far?

Rebecca: Yes, we're in the process of adopting.

Jeri: You are?

Rebecca: Yeah.

Jeri: You're going to adopt a . . .

Rebecca: A girl.

Jeri: There'll be another female.

Rebecca: [Laughs] Oh, definitely. Or going to try to anyway.

Ivan: Do you think that you get enough from them?

Rebecca: Oh, yeah, certainly.

Ivan: Okay, so, they're not treating you badly?

Rebecca: No, no.

Ivan: Well, it must be hard if you have these two smart guys . . .

[Rebecca breaks in before Ivan can finish the sentence.]

Rebecca: I just send them to Dan when they ask questions. One of the things I always thought I would do when they first started school is I'd get out the books and have all the answers for them. Right away, in first grade, they were already asking questions I had no answers for. So, Dad's been able to keep up with them so far.

Ivan: Rebecca, does the school know how smart Steve is?

Rebecca: They've tested him enough times.

Ivan: And they've concluded also that he's smart? Is it in his file?

Rebecca: All of his tests . . . I don't know if you guys have access to that . . .

Jeri: No.

Rebecca: But they have him at high-school level. He made the statement to me last year, "Mom, when do I go to school and learn something?"

Ivan: Are they treating him like a smart person?

Rebecca: No, because he doesn't produce.

Ivan: Like he says, he's bored, and so he doesn't . . .

Steve: I'm bored.

Rebecca: He doesn't produce. He had a science test, didn't do any of the assignments . . .

Steve: Didn't study at all. And I aced it, 100%.

Rebecca: He didn't open his book once. And he was the only one in his class that got 100%.

Steve: It was a simple test, and it was the semester test.

Jeri: I'm getting very confused listening. He said it was a simple test.

[Again, Jeri is trying to slow the process down so that everyone can keep up with the complexity of the dialogue, the paradoxical situations represented by the new information.

At this point we are comfortable with the fact that we have been accepted as trustworthy enough so that the family is sharing with us many of their concerns without fear that we are judging these concerns in a way that will be a detrimental to them. They have responded to our attempts to respect their views and to accept them in their own right.]

Ivan: So why bother?

Jeri: Oh, is that it? Is that the piece I'm missing? Why bother? I've never been that smart, so I wouldn't know.

Ivan: I haven't either. I'm guessing.

[We are not only sharing our own process, but we are sharing our interpretation of Steve's process so he can give us feedback about how he feels about what we think.]

Rebecca: I guess you guys are being hard on yourselves too [laughs].

Ivan: It's contagious.

Jeri: Is that what happened? We just caught it?

[This is not a conscious ploy on our part. We both rather spontaneously fell into this self-effacing state. It often happens when we allow ourselves to be immersed in a conversation and let the full impact of a belief system wash over us that we become a part of it for a while. It means to us that we are in a between experience with this family in that we are not holding ourselves outside of the dialogue or evaluating them on the basis of an objectifying set of criteria. We have taken on some of their meanings and have responded as such.]

Rebecca: I always had to study.

Dan: [To Steve] Do you feel that its kinda "why bother"? Are those the words that you'd use?

Steve: Hmm?

Dan: I mean, that you know that you can do real good and . . .

Steve: Well, if it cuts into my own time. During school time I'll do things, but if it cuts into my own time, why bother?

Ivan: So he would use that phrase?

Rebecca: I think there's also another element. I think he's also afraid that he will fail, too. He's never failed in the sense of trying hard at something.

Ivan: I'm sorry Rebecca that's very confusing for me. If somebody is afraid of failing . . .

[Ivan can now ask questions that are about Rebecca's views, and he can expect to get a response that is not screened by suspicion or a view to having to protect her son from an outside hostile source. It feels like we are in a genuine dialogue in which the clients feel they are being heard and considered from their perspectives.]

Rebecca: Yeah, then they don't try.

Ivan: But then, if they don't try, they don't fail?

Rebecca: But it's . . . they never think, "Well, I tried my best".

Ivan: So, they don't think they've failed, only the school would say: "You've failed."

Rebecca: Yeah. I mean, I'm talking about just in this personal sense.

Ivan: [To Steve] Did you understand that?

Steve: Uh huh. It was pretty close to the . . .

Rebecca: To the truth?

Steve: Yeah, the truth. Yeah, that's a way of saying it.

Jeri: Mom really understands you, doesn't she?

Steve: Mmmm. Sometimes.

Jeri: Sometimes Mom understands you.

Rebecca: There are times I don't.

Jeri: Does Dad understand you sometimes too?

Steve: Well, it's true everybody in the family can be a little impatient with me sometimes. I think, of all of them, Dad's the closest to me. In being close, I mean, . . . he doesn't say much to me but . . .

Jeri: But what?

Steve: I don't know. But in actual personality I guess I'm closer to him.

Jeri: You're closer to him in actual personality even though he doesn't say a lot? He sure is looking proud of you right now. You were saying that he was closest to you, and he's got a big, proud smile on his face.

[The above dialogue went from talking about Rebecca's hypothesis of Steve's fear of trying in order to avoid a sense of failure to a conversation about the shared identity between Steve and his father. This dialogue solidifies our budding belief that there is much love, compassion, and caring in this family. They are also aware of shared identities and differences.]

Ivan: What about you, Tim? How close do you think Dad and Steve are?

Tim: I don't play with Steve much cause he likes to jump on me all the time.

Ivan: Is he too big to jump on you?

Tim: Yeah. Well, he . . . when it comes to smart . . . well, we're just alike, but . . .

Ivan: When it comes to smart you're alike?

Tim: Yeah. But he never thinks smart unless it's at school and he's learning.

Jeri: He doesn't think smart?

Ivan: I didn't quite get that.

Tim: He doesn't like to use his brain. Only when he wants to, only when he needs to.

Jeri: So, he doesn't use his brain in school?

Ivan: You think he has control of that?

Tim: Yeah.

Ivan: You do? [To Steve] You think you have control over when you think smart and when you don't?

Steve: I'm usually too busy trying to stay away from a fight or just save myself from getting beat up. I don't have any time to think of schoolwork.

Ivan: So it's pretty scary?

[We learn for the first time that Steve spends most of his time at school being scared and finding ways to avoid being beaten up by other boys. It seems that most of the time he is acting out of fear. This is very different to acting from a position of being emotionally disturbed. His world view is that school is a dangerous place. Thus, his actions are syntonic with his world view.]

Steve: Yeah. When I have to go out, I have to tie down all my things. I have to tie them in the classroom at my desk because people go through there and ransack my things.

Ivan: You mean they kick you out of the room?

Steve: Then I have to go out and I have to go out with the teachers into the halls where they watch the other guys. So, I always have to be right beside the teachers. Because if I'm left alone in a classroom, they'll kill me.

Ivan: They'll kill you?

Steve: Well, pretty close to it. They do some pretty gruesome things to me. I've been hit, punched, kicked, knocked over . . .

Ivan: Nobody there to protect you?

Steve: Huh, uhh.

Ivan: Do you tell anybody?

Steve: I tried once.

Ivan: . . . about how dangerous it is . . .

Steve: . . . but the bell rang and I had to go to the classroom.

Jeri: [To Steve] Can I interrupt you a minute?

Steve: Yeah.

Jeri: Dan, have you heard this before?

Dan: Yeah, I have.

Jeri: Okay. I wasn't sure if you had.

Dan: I think that for Steve that's a real thing. That's really how he feels. Kind of a spooky thing.

Ivan: Have you ever been picked on yourself, Dan?

Dan: No, I don't think so.

Ivan: You haven't had that experience, then?

Dan: Nah, I wouldn't say so.

Ivan: So you wouldn't know what it's like to be that scared?

Dan: I don't think I'd know what it's like to be that scared, but I think I'd know what it is to be, oh, kind of, what would I say, marginally popular or something like that, or a little different, you know.

Ivan: A little different.

[By repeating one line of the dialogue we punctuate the idea we are repeating, and in addition we find that sometimes we can help clients stay with that thought or come back to it if their mind is going too fast. Again, it is a way of slowing things down so everyone can keep up with the thoughts, ideas, and feelings of everyone else. We hope the family will learn to do this and slow themselves down and, thus, communicate more clearly.]

Jeri: You know what that's like?

Dan: Yeah. But I would have to say that my experience has a different kind of coping to it.

Ivan: How is it different?

Dan: Well, I guess in my growing up what I did was I searched out other people that were kind of different, kind of off from the main track, and we kind of chummed around together, kind of protected ourselves. All in all, it came out just a real good experience.

[Jeri is looking for a symmetrical experience between father and son to continue to build the hypothesis about shared attributes in the family. Not finding it in this area, Ivan looks to build on the complementary aspects of the relationship.]

Ivan: Did you live in one place most of your childhood?

Dan: Yeah.

Ivan: Has Steve?

Dan: No.

Ivan: [To Steve] Do you guys move around?

Steve: Yeah.

Ivan: Do you think that would make it harder for you to find a group like your Dad was able to find?

Steve: I don't know. I've always adjusted to school or they've adjusted to me. I at least had a few friends. Here I have a few friends, but the problem is now that I'm changing classes all the time it seems that when I get a friend they get taken out of the class. They get their schedules changed. It's like the administration wants me to stay away from these people.

[By this point in the interview, we have the impression that our efforts to bend towards the family members and to personify that we care about their beliefs and dilemmas has been received by them. It seems, especially from Steve, that he is now able to actually tell us what he is preoccupied with, namely his fears about being alone without friends.]

Ivan: You mean they're taking them out of the class for you?

Steve: Well, it always seems like I . . . well I had this real good friend and they, . . . they, . . . I have one class with him and I had another one. They took him out of that class. And I had another one, and they took him out of that class, and I don't really have any other friends so I just try to survive.

[We could confront what seems like paranoid feelings, but to what end? This would have been a moment, from a traditional perspective, to view what Steve is saying as pathological. By letting Steve go on we come to some much more important feelings.]

Jeri: I'm feeling really sad. I wonder if anyone in the family is?

Ivan: I'm feeling really mad.

Jeri: You're feeling mad?

Rebecca: I'm feeling mad, too.

Jeri: You're feeling mad, too? How about you, Dan?

Dan: Well, I'm feeling sad.

[Expressing our genuine feelings of the moment in therapy is our way of connecting with the family members. It is about our internal experience

of the moment. A way to use ourselves. It is a way of creating a state of inclusion in the between.]

Jeri: [To Dan] You're feeling sad? That's what I thought. I was going to ask if you felt sad. You said you felt some of the other things that Steve's felt. So, I wondered if you also felt very sad like Steve? Like I think Steve is feeling now.

Dan: Hmm. Well the feeling of sadness that I have is sadness of perception. Because I know that there's just a whole lot of people that would really like to be Steve's friend.

[Jeri re-establishes the linkage of shared experience between Dan and his son. This is how we help family members in the confirmation of their relationships.]

Ivan: [To Dan] Excuse me a minute. Could you look at Steve when you say that? Steve, could you look at your Dad, because you might miss what he's trying to tell you.

[We have found that in addition to allowing people to hear each other's words better, making eye contact increases the intensity of their feelings for and about each other. It is a way to demonstrate to the family how they can practise emotional connectedness and inclusion.]

Dan: I just know that there's a lot of people that would like to be your friend, Steve. You know you really have something to offer.

Ivan: Whoops, he looked away at that. Do you think he feels he has nothing to offer?

[This intense contact can be more difficult for some people than others. We feel that helping Steve to experience the deep compassion and empathy his father wants to share with him may be worth the perseverance.]

Dan: Yeah, I think that's how he feels.

Jeri: Could you try again, Dan, and see if you can get him to stay with your eyes?

Dan: I really do think, Steve, that you have so many wonderful things to offer. You know, you think an entirely different way than all of us. Well, isn't that something to offer?

[We hear from the father that he believes his son is unique and different, and he frames this difference in positive terms.]

Steve: Yeah.

Dan: Well, just think of all those kids. You'll come up with a different idea . . .

Ivan: [To Steve] Look at your Dad.

[Steve now looks at his father more intently and with more warmth.]

Dan: . . . and they'll think, Gee, why didn't I think of that? That's a kind of an interesting way to look at something. Don't you think?

Steve: Problem is, Dad, that my ideas are so out of their fund. They don't accept them.

Ivan: The problem I have is that I haven't heard you say anything odd yet.

Steve: Well, when I'm talking to adults it's not that bad.

Ivan: Maybe you're an adult person?

Steve: Well, at least I can associate with them in an intellectual way. Well, what happens is people think I must be showing off because when I'm around them, I'll use a word that they'd never think of or don't know what it means, and they think that I'm trying to show off. So they don't like me.

Ivan: [To Tim] Just a moment. How is it going? Were you going to say something when Steve was talking about having conversations with adults?

Jeri: Ivan, we didn't ask Tim whether he felt sad or mad.

Ivan: That's right. Let's go back.

Tim: About what?

Jeri: About Steve.

Tim: [In an almost inaudible voice] Well, it's just that he doesn't like to express or show that he's someone special. Every time he makes excuses that he's a terrible person. Almost everybody in the whole school likes him.

Jeri: Almost everybody in the whole school likes him?

[This line was said with a great deal of drama. First of all, because Jeri is genuinely surprised and wants to show it, and second of all, because the family's affect is rather flat and reserved. Yet, we hear Tim, like his father, saying positive things about Steve. Their flat affect is in juxtaposition to the enthusiastic things they are saying about Steve. By becoming a little dramatic, Jeri is offering the family another option for expressing meaning.]

Tim: Well, it seems like it.

Jeri: It seems like it to you. [To Steve] Did you see him saying that to you?

Steve: Yeah.

Ivan: [To Steve] He thinks you're very special.

Steve: Well, I know. He might be a little different. He hasn't been through junior high. I don't know—that might be some excuse.

Jeri: He must have some reason for saying that almost the whole school likes you.

Steve: Either they are neutral or they hate me.

Ivan: Wait a minute, he says the whole school likes you.

Tim: Or everybody knows him.

Ivan: [To Tim] How about you? Do you like him?

Tim: Yeah.

Ivan: [To Steve] I think he likes you.

Steve: Of course, everybody knows me.

Ivan: I think he likes you.

Steve: Nobody forgets me.

Jeri: Steve, Tim said he likes you.

Steve: Probably.

Ivan: Probably.

Steve: Of course we have our fights and feuds.

Ivan: Of course, but that doesn't mean he doesn't like you.

Jeri: Brothers are supposed to have their fights and feuds. That's how they practise.

Steve: I mean everybody has their arguments.

Dan: Timmy. You said you think that the whole school knows him, kind of like he's famous or something?

Tim: Yeah.

Steve: Probably more infamous than famous.

Tim: Maybe he's famous because he's weird and stuff.

Steve: I'm different.

Tim: But at least he's known.

Ivan: You know, I believe everything Steve says.

Jeri: Yes.

Ivan: That he is so much smarter than other kids his age. I believe that 12-year-olds wouldn't have a chance to understand him.

Jeri: They wouldn't know that word "infamous".

Ivan: I've never heard a 12-year-old say: "I'm infamous." That's such a big idea to know the difference between famous and infamous. I'm absolutely overwhelmed.

[Rather than argue with Steve as most people might, Ivan stays with the positive reframing we have committed ourselves to. It seems to be an easier way for Steve to hear the compliment. And that is okay with us for now. Besides, we are sure that he is a pro at arguing. We have no chance of winning if we go up against him.]

Steve: I do know a lot more, and for some people I'm the first one they're going to try to study with.

Ivan: I have a feeling life is going to get better.

Jeri: Oh-h-h, the first one they're going to study with.

[And indeed! Steve is going to join us now with the positive ideas instead of fighting with us over whether he is okay or not.]

Steve: And then there are the majority of the people who are more than neutral. I mean, they might hear my name here and there, but they don't really know me. Then there's the other side. And those are the people, certain classes have certain of these people, especially, it's usually the classes I'm good in.

Ivan: I was wondering something.

Jeri: Okay, because I'm trying to be patient. Go ahead.

Ivan: I just wanted to acknowledge how much courage Tim has in bringing up all of these things. It takes a tremendous amount of courage.

[Tim is easily overlooked. We do not want to leave him out. He has been a valuable resource for us, and we want him to know it.]

Jeri: I'm glad you went first because I definitely agree with you.

Ivan: I just wanted that on the table.

Jeri: I need to go back. I said I felt sad and Dan talked about his sad feelings. I don't know whether anybody knows why you [meaning Ivan] and Mom got mad. Steve or Tim, do you have any idea? Why did your Mom feel mad when your Dad was feeling sad?

[We have some important threads to go back to. We feel that we have enough information now to be able to weave these threads about the pattern of the fabric of the family. We also feel that we have developed enough trust with Steve to elicit genuine feelings, different from the ones we might have elicited earlier in the process.]

Steve: Well, she's known me since I was a little baby. Parents like to be protectors. She wants to try and fight my battles, and, right now, I'm going through adolescence. So, I'm trying to grow up, and I'm being restrained a little bit. Sometimes I just, I'm not sure what I think, I just kind of lose my head, and I kind of go wild, I just . . .

Jeri: . . . like a person being restrained from growing up.

Steve: Yeah, I don't think very clearly or rationally. I just kind of don't put my head on straight. You know, say things I would never even mean to say.

Ivan: Is that adolescence?

Steve: I don't know.

Jeri: Is that adolescence or is that being restrained from growing up?

[We are asking for such distinctions in the hope of learning about Steve's theory of what is going on with him. To what extent is he, as a 12-year-old *male, beginning to struggle with issues of individualism, autonomy, and self-sufficiency?]*

Steve: It might be a mixture. It's probably more adolescence than being restrained.

Ivan: So, Mom is protecting you?

Steve: Yeah.

Ivan: Does that mean that's part of restraint?

Steve: By some people's standard, they'd be calling me over-sheltered.

Jeri: Over-sheltered? Okay.

[Steve is demonstrating that he has thought about these ideas. He has an ability to reflect on the relative merits of his ideas about himself and his relationships. This does not seem to be subject matter that a seriously emotionally disturbed adolescent would be preoccupied with.]

Ivan: Maybe your Mother still thinks she has a 12-year-old that she's raising, and she doesn't realize she has an 18-year-old.

Steve: Well, I'm not emotionally ready.

Jeri: Not emotionally ready for what?

Steve: Well, for living on my own or anything.

Jeri: Oh, okay, oh good . . .

Steve: Well, what happened is, in grade school, you know, jumping from 6th grade to 7th grade, it's like trying to jump up a 40-foot wall. You've got to be really determined to go up it.

[Steve continues to impress us with his ability to be self-reflective and thoughtful about his own experiences and his own development. He is exceptionally articulate for a 12-year-old child.]

Jeri: Yes.

Steve: In grade school they just had mock fights and stuff, you know, nothing bad—they'll say things to you—it won't be that bad. And you think that alcohol and drugs are a real far-off thing, and then when you get into junior high you've always got this stuff around. You've got people actually wanting to throw you into walls.

Jeri: Thrown into walls because . . . ?

Steve: Because they didn't like me. I mean, they don't really have any reason. They'll just go violent.

Ivan: So who's there to protect you?

Steve: Nobody.

Ivan: Your Mom protects you at home. Can she protect you elsewhere?

Steve: She hopes she can, but she can't.

[We have here a good example of what happens to a male child as he has experiences with other males away from home and away from the nurturing of his mother. It gets dangerous in the world, and his ability to cope with it is questionable. He seems to come from a home where there is no violence and where his being different is accepted. This is not the case in the unprotected world of school.]

Rebecca: I wish I could.

Ivan: Really, is that a tough job?

Rebecca: [With tears in her eyes] Oh, yeah. It's hard to let him go.

Ivan: To not be able to protect him in public?

Rebecca: Oh, sure. I realize that's part of our struggle right now. Stevie used to be someone who was very easy to take care of, to fight his battles for him and stuff. I can share an incident with you. I'm beginning to recognize that part of that is just natural pulling away. He's growing up.

[Rebecca has let us know how hard letting-go is for her by using the diminutive, "Stevie". Here we have an example of a mother who is having to struggle with letting her 12-year-old male son separate from her. It is a self-effacing experience for the mother, and probably a premature experience for the son, who feels the cultural pressure to separate but does not have the emotional maturity to carry it off.]

Jeri: Ouch!

[Jeri responds to Rebecca with compassion in a way that is open and sensitive and leaves room for humour.

We are now at a point in the interview where we are no longer struggling for understanding about this family because we are completely immersed with them in their experience. We are in that between where the differentiation between who is inside and who is outside is not important. What is important is the genuineness of the contact of the moment and the confirmation derived from that feeling of being inclusive. It is a state of having reconciled the contraries so that we can accept them and they us in all our wholeness in the present. We are in an I–Thou connectedness.]

Rebecca: He bought a little magnifying glass and took it to school. A kid took it away from him, and Stevie wasn't able to get it back. My natural inclination would be, let's get the boy on the phone, let's call the parents, let's get hysterical, let's get upset. What I did instead was I gave it back to Stevie. I said, Stevie, you're going to have to figure this one out.

Jeri: Is that right?

Rebecca: I thought that was really a big deal for me. Because it wasn't what I wanted to do.

Jeri: It was a big deal.

Rebecca: Yeah, it was.

Jeri: I'm impressed. But that must be hard for you as a mother.

Rebecca: Yes, because it's not normal for me to do that.

Jeri: Did anybody else know it was a big deal?

Rebecca: I think Stevie did, because the next day he processed what he was going to do about the situation. I was able to trust him enough to figure it out himself. He went up to the kid, and he gave him a couple of options. He can either give it back to me or he can give it to the vice-principal.

Steve: I said, either you give it to me, you let me look in your locker, or I'll have the vice-principal look through your locker. So you know, then he said that this was all a joke, and he gave it to me.

Rebecca: He was able to process it himself. I felt really good about it. I told him so, too.

Jeri: Do you think Dan knew what a big deal that was for you to be able to let go of Steve?

[We want to make sure that Rebecca is getting enough support to carry through with this difficult task of letting go of her first child.]

Rebecca: I think he knows that. He's the one who's been trying to tell me I should [laughing].

Jeri: I see.

Rebecca: It's very hard. It's real hard. I don't know, I've never had a teenager before. I don't know what I'm supposed to do. And I recognize that there's that pulling away, but there's still that wanting to nurture and wanting to be nurtured. And I don't know where the line is on that.

Jeri: That's tough.

Rebecca: Especially when kids pick on him.

Ivan: [To Steve] Did you know it was tough on Mom?

Steve: Yeah, it's probably extremely hard.

Ivan: More tough on her than on you?

Steve: I wouldn't say that. I'd say it's probably mixed. I mean I can be real cruel to people and I can be real cold. Okay, I can be real cold on the outside and kind of mean. Try to test me, and I'll bounce it right back at you. I don't let anybody mess with me, even though I can't do anything about it. I turn people away.

Ivan: You turn people away when you get cornered? Is it effective?

Steve: Mmm. Not always.

Jeri: [To Ivan] Are you as impressed as I am that he was aware that it was difficult for Mom? I usually don't come across 12-year-old kids who are striving for their independence and know it's difficult on their Moms.

Ivan: I was struck by that too. I'm wondering if other 12-year-olds don't understand him, if his parents also might not understand him, because he can take both sides.

Jeri: Yes.

Ivan: He's not acting like adolescents who take one side and fight to the death. Steve says: "Well, I understand that it's tough on you and it's tough on me." He understands all this. He says: "I'm not emotionally ready!"

Jeri: And he says: "She's restraining me, but I'm trying."

[This is an example of a spontaneous reflection between us about Steve and the dilemma of growing up and being different. We are discussing the self-reflectivity of this 12-year-old and we are confirming, but with a positive tone, how different he is.]

Ivan: [To Rebecca] Is this difficult for you?

Rebecca: Oh yeah, very much so, because in some ways you can talk to him, and he's been like this for years. He's had this way of processing.

[In our language, it seems Rebecca is saying that Steve has been able to be self-reflective for years. He knows how to sort things out and to remark on his process of doing the sorting.]

Ivan: Is this a congratulations?

Rebecca: Yeah, it's a real healthy thing.

Ivan: I don't know if he [Steve] knows it. [To Steve] Did you know that she's saying something very complimentary to you?

Steve: [Nods his head yes] Mmmm.

Ivan: I just wanted to post you on that. She's about to say something very nice.

Steve: Well, uhh, well, I don't know.

Ivan: Well, let's let her say it and see if you can hear it from her.

Steve: Speak!

Rebecca: Well . . .

Ivan: Can you look at her?

Rebecca: One of the things is about when we're talking and the walls are down. It's like talking to a friend, like an adult, and that's real good because I don't have to talk to you like a child.

Steve: Yeah. You usually try to talk to me like a child.

Rebecca: There are times when I do because you're acting like one.

Steve: Usually. Usually!

Ivan: You're saying he's both?

Rebecca: Oh yeah. And I think he gets really confused. And I never know which one it will be.

Jeri: How about you? Do you get confused?

Rebecca: Oh, definitely.

Jeri: You get confused. [To Dan] How about you? Do you ever get confused?

Dan: Oh, yes.

Jeri: Tim, how about you? Do you get confused about when he's being an adult and when he's being a kid?

Tim: Yeah.

Jeri: All right. So, all four of you are having some confusion about this. Sounds like adolescence to me.

[Jeri's conversation with all four family members is about the solidity of their identity as a family. They have established that there are close connections among them as they readily describe their feelings about themselves and each other. Their ability to articulate all this is impressive and not what we would have expected of a family who had been described with such negative attributions. We are surprised at the depth of the trust and mutual respect that is being demonstrated here.]

Rebecca: Yes. That's what they keep telling me. One thing that he said was about when he was sharing with Jon. He was angry towards me, and he came home, and said: "Mom, I'm really concerned about you now because I've shared some things that might put you in jail." I said: "Well, if I need to go to jail then I need to be there, and Jon will be able to discern if I'm doing something unhealthy." And I think basically all he was doing was saying he was angry at me.

Ivan: There are no skeletons in the closet?

Rebecca: I don't have any. I think there is anger between us. 'Cause he's trying to pull away, and I'm not necessarily letting him.

Steve: I can't say anything against that, that's the truth. I said that.

[Remember that the prospect of mother going to jail was brought up by Jon in his presentation of the family. We are satisfied that we can take at face value what Rebecca has to say about this. We did not have to act like detectives trying to expose a crime. This issue was brought up spontaneously by Rebecca and was innocuous.]

Ivan: But it is also a question of whether Jon is trustworthy?

Rebecca: Yeah, it was part of it too.

Steve: Well, I stepped out on a limb and it hasn't broken yet.

Jeri: All right! You mean that you told something to Jon which you thought could send your Mom to jail, but what turned out to be most important is how your Mom and Jon handled the information?

Steve: Yeah. It's worked out so far, so I'm going to see how long it will go.

Jeri: You picked a very good limb to step out on.

Steve: I hope.

[Jon is now brought into this. Steve is able to talk about the positive experience he is having with Jon.]

Jeri: I hope. How will you know how far out you can go?

Steve: I hate playing it by ear, but I guess I'm gonna have to do it.

Jeri: You hate playing it by ear? When you took your first step, how did you decide that that was a good limb to step out on?

Steve: I didn't know. I thought I was going to fall.

Jeri: You backed into it again, huh?

Steve: Well, I didn't back up from it though. I was going to and then I just decided "Why am I doing this?" So I just kind of stayed out there.

Jeri: You just stayed out there?

Ivan: Same thing Dad described half an hour ago.

[Continuity in a conversation is a prerequisite to a genuine dialogue. This means we have succeeded in creating a safe-enough environment. Steve's metaphor allows us to see that he trusts Jon too.]

Steve: That's rare. I usually get dropped right on my face. Taking unneeded risks.

Jeri: Do you think that Jon was a part of that limb?

Steve: Oh yeah. I was thinking, why am I doing this? I didn't even know I had taken a jump. Then I jumped off it, and then I thought, oh no, where am I now? If I'm going to do something, I have to do it real quick, or I'll get scared, and I won't do it.

Ivan: So you have to climb back onto the limb? If you stand there you'll back off. Is that right?

Steve: Definitely. I have to do things quick, or I'll start having second thoughts.

Ivan: Are you doing it quick now with Jon?

Steve: I'm already on the limb. I'm not about to back off.

Jeri: [To Steve] Would you do me a favour? Would you take a look at your Dad's face real quickly?

Steve: I'm out that far [gesturing with his hands spread far apart]. I'm gonna see. I know that part's stable.

Jeri: That part's stable [gesturing with her hands].

Rebecca: I like hearing that, too, because he's been approaching Jon very cautiously.

Jon: I like hearing that, too.

Steve: At least I got out there [laughing tentatively].

Jeri: You sure did. You got lots of smiles, too. Would you look around the room? Look at this group. Your Dad is smiling, your Mom is smiling, and Jon is smiling.

Steve: Good.

Jeri: Good.

Ivan: How are you doing, Tim? Are we paying too much attention to him?

Tim: Nooo.

Ivan: I remember you mentioned that he likes the attention.

Tim: Yeah.

Ivan: And you seem very quiet and mellow over there.

Tim: Yeah. I think he's just making up stories to get attention. And it makes me jealous.

[These two children continue to impress us with their grasp of their emotional reactions to one another. They are articulate about their feelings in ways many children, especially males, are not.]

Steve: The story I just told?

Jeri: [To Tim] And it makes you jealous?

Steve: What I said right here?

Tim: Yeah.

Ivan: He says he's jealous.

Tim: Well, most of it's true.

Ivan: Most of it.

Jeri: Do you think Steve ever gets jealous of you Tim?

Tim: Yeah. He gets jealous of me.

Jeri: When do you think he gets jealous of you?

Tim: Well, . . . I don't know. Well, . . . I know a lot of kids at school do.

Jeri: When do you think your brother feels jealous of you?

Tim: Well [long pause] . . . that I get to do a lot of things that Steve doesn't get to do.

Jeri: Like what? What do you get to do?

Tim: I get the mail. But he doesn't really care about that.

Ivan: What does he care about that you do that he's jealous of?

Tim: I don't know.

Steve: Well, okay . . .

Jeri: I think he wants to tell you.

Steve: Well, if I'm ever trying to do something with my Dad, I'll usually say something that I shouldn't, and that's it. Me and Dad will get in a yelling contest. Or not yelling actually, it's more like a discussion. Of course I go out of the house and I couldn't care less. But Tim, he seems to in-fight, he seems to worm his way in somehow.

Jeri: Worm his way in?

Steve: I guess I'm jealous of Tim because he knows what to say around Dad and when to say it. I'll open my mouth and say something really stupid. Most of the time I try to sell myself a lot on the idea that I don't care. I guess I really do care.

[Steve offers another amazing self-reflection about his feelings. He is able to articulate the internal struggle he has about a typical adolescent issue of caring and not appearing to care.

These children are being exceptionally candid. For our part, we are fully appreciating the conversation about similarities and differences and the reconciliation of and respect for differences.

We are embracing contraries and tolerating these contraries and un-certainties long enough to have genuine I–Thou contact.]

Ivan: So he [Tim] knows how to do things and stay in a good place with your Dad.

Steve: Uh huh.

Ivan: He has a very important skill.

Steve: Yeah. I'm not sure what you'd call it. You might call it deception, you might call it kind of lying [laughs]. He'll always find the solution, even if it's something there is one-in-a-million chance that it would work. He always finds his way into something.

Jeri: Do you think Dad is a little surprised at what you said, or very surprised?

Steve: I don't know. [Sigh] You'll have to ask him.

Dan: I am a little surprised, but not entirely surprised. I think it's part of what we were talking about earlier, about how you felt you were mostly like me. But I like to do things like pound nails, fix things, and your brother really likes that too. So that lends itself, doesn't it, to that earlier thing about jealousy?

Steve: Yeah.

Jeri: [to Steve] Do you like to do things that they like to do, the two of them?

Steve: Well, we talk. Sometimes I'll have a question and, the two of us, we'll have a talk.

Jeri: The two of you?

Steve: Yeah. We'll talk intellectual ideas. I'll ask him a question and it will come into a conversation. I'll tell him what I think on different theories.

Ivan: So you are both theory men?

Steve: Yeah. Sometimes we talk. Most of the time I usually think of the theories, and he usually just knows a lot of information. I usually judge on different things because I guess you could call me a budding poet.

Ivan: A budding poet!

Steve: Yeah. I like writing poems and stories.

Ivan: You do?

Steve: Yeah, I'm a pretty good author.

Jeri: You know I always think it's interesting the way that families work out. One kid gets a father that likes to do stuff, and one kid gets the father that likes to talk about stuff.

Ivan: This family has one father that likes to do both.

Jeri: Yes, and does both too.

Steve: I know, but he actually probably does more of the other things. Occasionally I can get him into a good discussion. We mainly agree on everything, so discussions are not real exciting.

Ivan: Is that right?

Steve: If you agree on things, discussions are not very exciting.

Ivan: Have you ever thought of writing poetry together?

Steve: I write better on my own, actually.

Ivan: What do you think it would be like to write a poem with your Dad?

Steve: I've never actually tried it. It might be different.

Ivan: How would you go about it?

Steve: [With hesitation] Well, I'd probably take one of my thoughts and then he can change words, put in more verses. Do anything he wanted to.

Jeri: [To Ivan] It sounds like Steve might give up the whole poem. Perhaps this is too difficult. Perhaps he could write one about his Dad instead? That might be easier, since he likes to do it alone.

Steve: Sometimes I just write something off the top of my head. I just sit there and it comes.

Jeri: I don't think Ivan is satisfied. I think he wants you to write with your Dad.

Ivan: [To Jeri] Tell you why. I'm getting the impression that the education of Steve goes on at home and not in school. And therefore, to write poetry together furthers the education and the relationship.

Jeri: I like that.

Ivan: [To Jeri] This is a family that is smarter about what it needs than is the school. So they have to keep educating at home with each other.

Jeri: [To Ivan] You know, I was listening to you talk about that, and I'm thinking that they just have a few more years to do that with Steve.

Ivan: When he gets to college he's going to have more requests to be studied with than he'll ever be able to fulfil.

Jeri: That's right.

Ivan: There'll be a waiting list. So they had better do this now while they can.

Jeri: I was feeling very glad that somebody else was going to be coming along that they could start educating. Another bright child [referring to the child they are hoping to adopt].

[We pause here to allow the family to think about what we are talking about. We then resume our dialogue with each other.]

Jeri: I keep thinking it's going to be very satisfying, fulfilling for Mom.

Ivan: Wouldn't it be mind-blowing if Steve and Dan wrote a poem and both took it to school to read. What do you think it would be like, for the school? That could educate the school about what happens when you are bored in school and not bored at home.

Steve: I did that. I wrote poems and gave them to my English teacher, and she's being pretty wild about it. She's saying, you're real good. In translation, she probably thinks I'm a genius [nervous laugh].

Ivan: Can they cope with geniuses at your school?

Rebecca: Not unmotivated ones. Motivated ones they probably can because they plug them into the system that's already there. Ones that haven't been motivated don't get into the special programs. You gotta be motivated first.

Ivan: I'm getting the impression that Steve is protecting himself about some very important things. He's very motivated in this conversation, but you seem to be protecting yourself from the outside world.

Steve: I like discussing, especially with adults.

Ivan: I'm impressed that he needs a mentor.

Jeri: Yes.

Steve: I like talking. I do better verbally.

Jeri: I'm impressed that he's sitting between two of them [Jon and Dan].

Ivan: There they are.

Rebecca: Can you remember one of your poems that you could tell them?

Steve: Oh yeah.

Tim: He has one about the turkeys being slaughtered.

Jeri: One about the turkeys being slaughtered.

Dan: It actually was an article instead of a poem that you published.

Steve: I was doing a project, and me and Randy, he's actually my best friend in school, wrote this article together about turkey slaughter on Thanksgiving. It was about Mr. Herbert McTurkey. He was protesting the turkey murders. He was out on the street protesting this ad for a turkey resort. This turkey resort would offer free rides on the train. What happened was they got the turkeys on the train, and cornered them, and they killed them.

Ivan: But they never returned.

Jeri: A resort is supposed to be a safe place.

[*What an incredible metaphor Steve created about his school experience. He is promised an education, but that is not what he got. It is not a safe enough place to learn. It is clear that Steve has a deep sense of mistrust about school. It is very hard for him to trust the outside world. It does not seem, however, that he mistrusts his parents. In fact, he exhibits a good deal of compassion for them.]*

Ivan: I'm still impressed with how proud Tim is of his brother.

Jeri: Tim has been so helpful.

Ivan: Well, you know we could go on for a long time, but I'm afraid we're going to have to take a break.

Jeri: I really enjoyed talking to you.

* * *

Reflecting with the family

Because this was a training workshop as well as a consultation, we asked the family to leave the room in order to organize our collective thoughts before ending. After about fifteen minutes, the family returned and we talked with them. The following is what transpired.

Jon: I came up with some things I want to share with you. I was impressed by your willingness to come in today and by some other things as well. I was very impressed by the tenderness that you show for each other, and the emotional support that you are able to provide for one another when you talk about issues. I was also aware that the family is going through some developmental changes now. Kids growing up, and a new child coming into the family. But all of you seem to be able to talk about those issues with courage and a great deal of support for each another.

    Steve, about the work that you and I are doing together, I'm aware that I'm seeing you now as a representative of the school, but I want to point out that I'm also available to see you independent of the school. We don't need to depend on the school, like during the summer.

Ivan: We came into this to try to be useful to Jon and to you through the work that Jon is doing with Steve. We'd like to acknowledge that we think that Jon is in a tough spot. We believe that you're a very caring family, and we think that you're going to continue to take care of one another. We also think the school as an institution is going to take care of itself. What the school provides Steve may or may not fit his needs. Jon is in the middle of this. A strong family and strong school system, and so we think he has a very delicate role to play. It is courageous of you, Jon, to continue to try to be helpful to both groups. [To the family and Jon] We are impressed with all of your courage.

Jeri: I hope this has been useful to you. I want you to know how helpful it has been to the audience in terms of learning about families. We greatly appreciate your coming and teaching us so much.

Rebecca: Well, one thing that I am feeling, and we were talking about upstairs. So many times we feel there is blaming. Our hearts have always been for these kids. They are our lives. Then when something goes wrong we think, What have I done wrong, what are we doing? Are we talking about some kind of dysfunction or something? Schools are really quick to pick up on it. It's like it's always the family that is at fault. We've always been real open to looking at our part. If there is something going on, we want to know about it so we can deal with it. It encouraged Dan and me that you see us. You see us as real people, and it made us feel like we are doing something right. Because that is the conviction of our hearts.

Jeri: I think you are doing lots of things right. You are special people.

Rebecca: It means a lot to us.

Ivan: We appreciate your feedback too. Is there anything that the rest of you would like to say to us?

Steve: I think I learned something.

Jeri: Anything you'd like to share?

Steve: I think that this has been interesting. I think I have learned something. I'm glad that I could help people who are learning things. It gave me a kind of different view. Even though we may have a crisis or two in the family now and then, it makes me think that we are pretty functional.

Ivan: Wow!

Jeri: [To Tim] How about you?

Tim: It was better than I thought it was going to be. I've never done it before, and I didn't know there was going to be this many people.

Jeri: Too many people.

Tim: I always forget. If you ask a question I would answer it. I forgot what it was I was going to say.

Jeri: I'll tell you what, if you ever remember what it is you were going to say, you can tell it to your brother, who will tell it to Jon, and it will get to us.

Ivan: Dan, would you like to say something about this experience before you leave?

Dan: Yeah, I wanted to ask you a question, Steve. I wondered how you felt when Jon made a neat offer to you about seeing you in a setting that was not just at the school. We've been talking before about the limb and how you felt that you had a conviction to go ahead with it, that you were feeling more and more trust. That's the word that I use. I think that's maybe what you're feeling. How did you feel about his suggestion, his offer?

Steve: Well, in the summer, I'll probably be on my own and not have that problem with popularity. I'll be with my family. My family is not my main troubles. Okay, how can I say this. I guess that emotionally I'm still a kid, but that intelligently, I am high-school level.

Jeri: Do you think that your Dad thinks that Jon could help you grow up emotionally?

Steve: What?

Jeri: Do you think your Dad would like you to see Jon in the summer?

Steve: Probably.

Jeri: That's what I think, too.

Ivan: I have a feeling that this is a private conversation.

Jeri: I agree with you.

Ivan: It should take place somewhere else.

Jeri: And what I felt was still a part of this process was whether Dad felt supportive of Jon. That question was still up in the air, and that was what I wanted to bring out. He said he thought Dad probably did want him to see Jon. There is a certain amount of allegiance that he has to Dad, so he has to know if it's okay.

Ivan: This might be like giving permission.

Dan: I think so.

Ivan: Wow! That's a big thing when a father gives his son permission to have a relationship with another man. That's a big move. That's courageous on the part of a father.

Jeri: Thank you very much. It was a pleasure to meet you.

Ivan: Thank you. Take care, and good luck on all your growing.

* * *

The audience responds

We had asked several members of the audience who were in our on-going training group to act as an observing team during the consultation interview. During the debriefing, we asked the observing team and Jon to give us their impressions of the family and of the process of the interview.

Ray: I think the family's feedback was a real testimony to your attention to what is working for them as a family: the positives of their lives together. They felt validated, supported, and normalized. I think they probably left feeling very good about themselves, empowered, and very different about this feedback versus that of the school and other people they have received feedback from in the past. So I think it was a very successful consultation interview.

Wolfgang: I was aware that many of us have a real hard time avoiding looking for pathology, looking for dysfunction, looking at the negative process of the family. I think Jon is between a rock and a hard place because he sees the family here, and the school has a different image of this family. This interview demonstrates that they are different from the stereotype. But how could Jon possibly convince the school of that? Steve's behaviour in school leads to their conclusion that the family must be dysfunctional.

Anything contrary would not be believed, because it does not fit standard theory.

Judith: It reminds me of our previous conversations about letting go of a hypothesis as if it were a dirty handkerchief. It was helpful to me to go through all the hypothesizing before the family arrived because, as I was watching the family, I could toss the dirty handkerchief away. We came up with a lot that didn't fit.

Ivan: It told us what our repertoire might be going into the interview. Then it opened the possibility of being complementary to our anticipations. When we hear new information from the family that doesn't fit, it's time to drop the dirty handkerchief. This family kept surprising me. By choosing to believe what the family told us, we were able to use that to develop a relationship with them. This does require that we drop the pathology model. But if you feel that your allegiance must be towards that model and you have pre-existing categories to put people into, then you won't drop the dirty handkerchief. You will try to disprove the family in order to hold constant the applied-science view.

Ray: We have thrown out a lot of dirty handkerchiefs. Assuming that therapy was continuing, I would have to develop a whole new set of hypotheses. Is it just as dangerous now to hypothesize?

Jeri: Yes. It would be the same process. We would still have to be prepared to throw away the dirty handkerchief and keep the clean ones.

Ivan: If we met with them again, they might surprise us with something new.

Jeri: I'm sure they would. There is no doubt in my mind. In a few weeks they might not be the same family we saw today.

Ivan: This is the reality we all constructed today with the audience. If we were to do a second interview without an audience, we might find that one of the significant issues of this interview was the audience, and that without an audience we would develop a different relationship, a different co-construction.

Jeri: In our first-year class, we do a three-session demonstration interview with a family. We then go on seeing them outside class, and then, at the end of the year, we bring them back to the class for another interview, so the class sees the differences that have taken place since then.

Nancy: I noticed that both of you reframed Steve's comments about himself in the beginning. His first comment about himself was that he was no good. You could see that his unattended view about himself was that he regarded himself poorly. The whole flow of the interview changed when you insisted on having positive regard for him. The family then followed suit.

Jeri: And about themselves too. They had more positive regard for themselves and each other.

Ivan: Mother was doing the same thing. She said: "I'm not as smart as the others."

Nancy: I believe they left with that more positive view of themselves, and I hope they can sustain it. The school might continue to encourage and reinforce the negative trend. But Jon, you get to continue the positive reframe with Steve.

Jon: A different way to have interviewed them would have brought out the negative attributes, like "I'm no good" or "I'm not smart". So, I think the school experiences that side of Steve. When Steve comes to school and says that stuff, he has convinced the school, and they respond that way.

Ivan: That is the problem of the school being in symmetry with the child and family. I wonder how different it would be if the school took a complementary position, like we took today? What if they refused to believe in his negativity and insisted that he was terrific, and was a poet, and a genius? They might be able to help him be more productive.

Wolfgang: I am interested in something I actually did not see today. What happens when the two of you disagree?

Jeri: We agree to disagree.

Wolfgang: What is it like when you agree to disagree?

Jeri: Many times when we are working with families we escalate our disagreements, amplify them, and really get into it. We do that in order to maintain genuineness and to highlight that it is possible to disagree.

Ivan: But our first job is to make it safe. So if we disagree and are working with a family that cannot disagree, then the first thing that one of us will do is ask the family if it is okay with them if we disagree, and would they let us know if they cannot handle it. Then we disagree and ask the family for feedback about our disagreement. How did you see this disagreement? What do you think we should do about this disagreement? This keeps us in relationship with the family and in the process.

* * *

After the feedback of the observing team, we opened the discussion to the entire audience. It became apparent to us during the debriefing that the family had an unmistakable impact on this audience. The family was seen as a very positive force in Steve's life. There was some confusion about how Steve could be experienced so differently in school from the way he came across in this interview. The family was seen through compassionate eyes by the audience. The hardness and cold clinical views had melted away in favour of warmth, compassion, and empathy for this family's struggle to get through life successfully. It was an experience of how a family can impact the therapists and transform their views and ways of constructing a deductive picture of a family based on theoretical premises. It was an experience of a moment in time when preconceived notions did not prevail but gave way to the actuality of the contact among people in interaction. It was what Buber referred to as a moment of grace—one that could not have been planned for or structured. It was an experience in the *between*. It was for us an experience along that narrow ridge (Friedman, 1991) of creating genuine contact among people.

We were impressed with the power of this experience to change the thinking of our fellow professionals and with their flexibility to experience change as they followed the process. In the face of a changing context, the audience responded to the family as they presented themselves and unfolded their story. The context was a very powerful shaper of meanings and was able to influence theories and beliefs of long standing. We are aware of how important it is for many professionals and institutions to hold on to their beliefs regardless of context as a way of ensuring certainty, continuity, and perceived stability.

CHAPTER SEVEN

Reflections

> There are two kinds of therapists, one who knows more
> or less consciously the kind of interpretation of dreams
> he will get; and the other, the psychologist who does not
> know. I am entirely on the side of the latter, who does
> not want something precise. He is ready to receive what
> he will receive. He cannot know what method he will use
> beforehand. He is, so to speak, in the hands of his
> patient.
>
> Martin Buber, *The Knowledge of Man*, 1965b, p. 37

To practice from an ethical perspective in family therapy, we must appreciate the dilemmas of our clients as genuine ones. In the family we presented in the previous chapter, the dilemmas included the mother's concern about the separation experience with her oldest son, the son's terrorizing experiences in school, the younger son's confusion about what makes his older brother "tick", and the father's dilemma of how to teach his oldest son to be a well-functioning adolescent in the world of interpersonal relationships. Our job was to create an atmosphere in which

113

these dilemmas could be expressed without the blame that Rebecca reported had been their experience with other professionals. To be heard as "real people" by human service professionals constituted a new and different experience for this family.

In order to communicate an ethic of care, therapists must suspend negative judgements about the family and listen to their perspective about their lives. It is important to find ways of offering feedback which are not foreign or noxious to a family, so that they are not relegated to an I–It status. Therapists are more likely to communicate an ethic of care with clients when they immerse themselves in a dialectic experience, one in which the reality of the family is accepted as authentic. When the authenticity of the beliefs of the family is respected, then a co-evolving process can occur. When that happens, a *between* is formed, and shared meanings can be developed and an atmosphere of mutuality can exist.

As we entered this interactive experience, we acknowledged our many preconceived ideas. These preconceived ideas were treated as hypotheses. They told more about ourselves, the therapist, and the audience than they did about the family. Hypotheses are more ephemeral than substantive or stable. From a collective point of view, "imagining the between" is a way of entering an experience believing that our imaginings help us find ways of deriving meanings from the experience. The concept implies that the best we can do as knowers is to be able to imagine our own beliefs and those of others. It implies that knowing is a way of attempting to diminish the tensions of uncertainty, but that knowing is not absolute. Rather, knowing is a state of believing, imagining, guessing, approximating, and projecting. Knowing is no more than experiencing the meanings we make from our experiences regardless of how organized or systematic the meaning-making process.

Like many others who experience crises of uncertainty, therapists who subscribe to a social construction perspective are in a continuous state of at least minor crises of uncertainty. By being able to live with the uncertainties that accompany a rejection of traditional psychological theories, social construction therapists must be ready to treat all experiences as novel experiences. The world of interaction is full of surprises for social construction therapists. There is never a dull moment, because the meaning-making is a product of the interaction itself. It is not predetermined.

As we have become more deeply involved in the philosophical and ethical issues of family therapy, we have realized the need to be acutely aware of the strings attached to the work we do. Those strings include who pays us, what relationship we have with referral sources, how we are perceived by the clients as collaborators or adversaries, and how our personal attitudes, values, and beliefs are complementary or symmetrical to those of the family and its individual members. The context we build with families depends upon how these attached strings play out in the course of the dialogue, and what consequences accrue from these strings. Therapy is a political process. There should be no illusion that therapy is an isolated experience independent of the rest of social, political, and economic life. We are part of the culture in which we live and work, as are the clients with whom we come into contact. We are embedded in our values and prejudices. We are not outside the social ecology. We are a part of a professional class and subclasses within the class. We stand for ideas, and practices, and personify them in the work we do. From an ethical perspective we must acknowledge all this to ourselves and then to those to whom we provide services. It is our obligation to incorporate that understanding in our work and to be authentic about it. If we promote a social construction metaphor, we must also realize that our beliefs and prejudices are a part of that which we participate in socially constructing. This can mean that we must continually acknowledge our limitations and the constraints on us when we are in the therapeutic milieu. Therefore, social construction thinking includes a self-reflectivity that acknowledges the limits of our thinking and acting in different contexts. There are those contexts—and schools may be an example—in which we could not have experienced the kind of interview we did with this family. It may not have been possible for us to have developed a mutuality of trust and positive regard because of the personal and political consequences. So we have to be content with the idea that only in certain contexts can a genuine dialogue evolve, and, even when all the necessary conditions are there, it may not evolve. The experience is produced in a state of grace. We may have to be grateful when it happens and not fall into the trap of applied science and believe that, if we could control enough of the conditions, we could make things happen when we want them to happen.

REFERENCES

Andersen, T. (1987). The reflecting team: Dialogue and meta-dialogue in clinical work. *Family Process, 26*: 415–428.

_____ (Ed.) (1991). *The Reflecting Team: Dialogues and Dialogues about the Dialogues.* New York: W. W. Norton.

Anderson, H., & Goolishian, H. (1988). Human systems as linguistic systems: Preliminary and evolving ideas about the implications for clinical theory. *Family Process, 27*: 371–393.

Arendt, H. (1977). *The Life of the Mind.* San Diego, CA: Harcourt Brace Jovanovich.

Bateson, G. (1972). *Steps to an Ecology of Mind.* New York: Ballantine Books.

_____ (1979). *Mind and Nature: A Necessary Unity.* New York: Dutton.

Bateson, G., & Bateson, M. K. (1987). *Angels Fear: Towards an Epistemology of the Sacred.* New York: Macmillan.

Berger, P., & Luckman, T. (1966). *The Social Construction of Reality.* Garden City, NY: Doubleday.

Boscolo, L., & Bertrando, P. (1993). *The Times of Time: A New Perspective in Systemic Therapy and Consultation* (transl. by Stephen Thorne). New York: W. W. Norton.

Boscolo, L., Cecchin, G., Hoffman, L., & Penn, P. (1987). *Milan Systemic Family Therapy: Conversations in Theory and Practice*. New York: Basic Books.

Bowen, M. (1976). Theory in the practice of psychotherapy. In: P. J. Guerin (Ed.), *Family Therapy: Theory and Practice*. New York: Gardner Press.

_____ (1978). *Family Therapy in Clinical Practice*. New York: Jason Aronson.

Buber, M. (1958). *I and Thou* (2nd edition) (transl. by R. G. Smith). New York: Charles Scribner's Sons.

_____ (1965a). *Between Man and Man*. New York: Macmillan.

_____ (1965b). *The Knowledge of Man: A Philosophy of the Interhuman* (transl. by M. Friedman & R. G. Smith). New York: Harper & Row.

_____ (1973). *Meetings*. LaSalle, IL: Open Court Publishing.

Capra, F. (1982). *The Turning Point: Science, Society and the Rising Culture*. New York: Simon & Schuster.

Cecchin, G., Lane, G., & Ray, W. (1992). *Irreverence: A Strategy for Therapists' Survival*. London: Karnac Books.

Dell, P. (1982). Beyond homeostasis: Toward a concept of coherence. *Family Process, 21*: 21—42.

Eliot, T. S. (1936). The love song of J. Alfred Prufrock. In: *Collected Poems 1909–1935*. New York: Harcourt, Brace.

_____ (1939). *Old Possum's Book of Practical Cats*. New York: Harcourt Brace Jovanovich.

Frankl, V. E. (1959). *Man's Search for Meaning: An Introduction to Logotherapy*. New York: Beacon Press.

Freud, S. (1895) (with Breuer, J.). *Studies on Hysteria. Standard Edition of the Complete Psychological Works of Sigmund Freud, Vol. 23* (pp. 209–254). London: Hogarth, 1975.

Friedman, M. (1985). *The Healing Dialogue in Psychotherapy*. New York: Jason Aronson.

_____ (1991). *Encounter on the Narrow Ridge: A Life of Martin Buber*. New York: Paragon House.

_____ (1993). Healing through meeting. My personal way into psychology. *Voices* (Spring): 10–17.

Gergen, K. (1985). The social constructionist movement in modern psychology. *American Psychologist, 40*: 266–275.

Gilligan, C. (1982). *In a Different Voice: Psychological Theory and Women's Development*. Cambridge, MA: Harvard University Press.

Goldner, V. (1988). Generation and gender: Normative and covert hierarchies. *Family Process, 27*: 17–32.

Hoffman, L. (1981). *Foundations of Family Therapy: A Conceptual Framework for Systems Change.* New York: Basic Books.

Inger, I. B. (1993). A dialogic perspective for family therapy: The contributions of Martin Buber and Gregory Bateson. *Journal of Family Therapy, 15:* 293–314.

Inger, I. B., & Inger, J. (1990a). The evolution of a multiperson therapeutic system. *Journal of Strategic and Systemic Therapies, 9:* 47–60.

_____ (1990b). *Co-constructing Therapeutic Conversations: A Consultation of Restraint.* London: Karnac Books.

Kenney, B. (1983). *Aesthetics of Change.* New York: Guilford.

Maturana, H. R. (1978). Biology of language: The epistemology of reality. In: *Psychology and Biology of Language and Thought: Essays in Honor of Eric Lenneberg.* New York: Academic Press.

Menninger, K. A., & Holzman, P. S. (1973). *Theory of Psychoanalytic Technique* (2nd edition). New York: Basic Books.

Polyani, M. (1969). *Knowing and Being.* Chicago: The University of Chicago Press.

Sampson, E. E. (1985). The decentralization of identity: Toward a revised concept of personal and social order. *American Psychologist, 40:* 1203–1211.

_____ (1988). The debate on individualism: Indigenous psychologies of the individual and their role in personal and societal functioning. *American Psychologist, 43:* 15–22.

Segal, L. (1986). *The Dream of Reality: Heinz von Foerster's Constructivism.* New York: W. W. Norton.

Shabatay, V. (1991). The stranger's story: Who calls and who answers? In: C. Witherell & N. Noddings (Eds.), *Stories Lives Tell: Narrative and Dialogue in Education.* New York: Teachers College Press.

Shaffer, P. (1974). *Equus.* New York: Avon Books.

Selvini-Palazzoli, M., Boscolo, L., Cecchin, G., & Prata, G. (1978). *Paradox and Counterparadox: A New Model in the Therapy of the Family in Schizophrenic Transaction.* New York: Jason Aronson.

Von Foerster, H. (1981). On constructing a reality. In: *Observing Systems.* Seaside, CA: Intersystems Publications.

Von Glasersfeld, E. (1979). The control of perception and the construction of reality. *Dialectica, 33:* 37–50.

_____ (1984). An introduction to radical constructivism. In: P. Watzlawick (Ed.), *The Invented Reality: How Do We Know What We*

Believe We Know? (Contributions to Constructivism). New York: W. W. Norton.

Walters, M., Carter, B., Papp, P., & Silverstein, O. (1988). *The Invisible Web: Gender Patterns in Family Relationships.* New York: Guilford.

Watzlawick, P. (Ed.) (1984). *The Invented Reality: How Do We Know What We Believe We Know? (Contributions to Constructivism).* New York: W. W. Norton.

Watzlawick, P., Jackson, D., & Beavin, J. (1967). *Pragmatics of Human Communication.* New York: W. W. Norton.

Watzlawick, P., Weakland, J., & Fisch, R. (1974). *Change: Principles of Problem Formation and Problem Resolution.* New York: W. W. Norton.

White, M. (1986). Negative explanations, restraint and double description: A template for family therapy. *Family Process, 25:* 169–184.

INDEX

"act of inclusion" [Buber], 12, 21, 48
aesthetics, 1, 3
Allegory of the Cave [Plato], 38
Andersen, T., 3, 24, 30, 32–35, 44, 117
Anderson, H., 41
Arendt, H., 40
attachment, 3, 8, 52
    of child to parents, 5–15
    between mothers and daughters, 8
    vs. self-containment, for male, 7
    vs. separation, 6, 7

Bateson, G., 19, 39, 41, 44
Bateson, M. K., 39
Beavin, J., 44
"being with ourselves" [Buber], 3, 45–
        46, 51, 58
"bending back to oneself", vs.
        "turning towards the other"
        [Buber], 49
"bending towards others" [Buber], 3,
        46–48, 51
Berger, P., 31
Bertrando, P., 20

"between", 3, 29, 48, 49, 50, 51, 69, 74,
        82, 88, 95, 112, 115
"identifying" [Buber], 48
"imagining", 115
binocular vision, principle of, 63
borderline personality, 14
Boscolo, L., 20, 34, 37, 44
Bowen, M., 10
Buber, M., 3, 5, 11, 12, 13, 21, 24, 27,
        28–32, 35, 41, 112, 113
    on ethically based therapy, 44–52

Capra, F., 37
care, ethic of, 50–51
Carter, B., 7
categorical thinking, 24
Cecchin, G., 34, 37, 41
character, sociopathic, 14
children, in hierarchy, 43
client:
    position, stigma attached to, 14
    shadow, 10
coherence, and family therapy, 18
collectivity, vs. individualism, 20

complementarity, 20, 86
    between aesthetics and
        psychotherapy, 1
    vs. individualism, 11
    vs. symmetry, 75, 115
connectedness:
    I–Thou, 29, 95
    practicing, 88
constructions of meanings, 47
consultation [clinical example], 53–112
control, field, 9, 10
countertransference, 12–13, 22
cultural discontinuity, 32–35

Dell, P., 18, 19
dependency, 10
dialogue, 51
    "genuine" [Buber], 31
    internal, 65
    uncertainty in, tolerating, 47
discontinuity, cultural, 32–35
double description, clarifying
        meanings through, 75

ego, and internal psychological
        changes, 19
Eliot, T. S., 1, 2, 53
Erickson, E., 6
ethic of care, 50–51
ethical perspective, practising from,
        37–52
ethically based therapy [Buber], 44–52
ethics, 1, 3, 38
    and anthropology, philosophy,
        performing arts, 3
    definition, 2
    personal, vs. certainty of
        "objectivity", 3
    of practice, 2
"experiencing the between" [Buber],
        3, 51
eye contact, 88

family:
    as system, 20
    therapy, change in, 17–20
fathers, and children, relationship
        between, 8

field control, 9, 10
Fisch, R., 44
Frankl, V. E., 37
Freud, A., 6
Freud, S., 6, 12
Friedman, M., 18, 27, 49, 52, 112
Fromm, E., 6

gender, 80
    and family therapy, 18
    issues, 20
generativity, and family therapy, 18
"genuine dialogue" [Buber], 31
Gergen, K., 31
Gilligan, C., 50–51
Goldner, V., 18
Goolishian, H., 41
Guntrip, H., 6

healing, and family therapy, 18
hierarchy, 24
Hoffman, L., 37, 44
Holzman, P. S., 12
Horney, K., 6

I–It, 42, 114
    attitude, 29, 45, 46, 49
    concept, 28
    and I–Thou, 30, 31, 44, 45, 51, 58
    relationship, 29, 30
I–Thou, 5
    attitude, 42, 45, 46, 49, 52
    concept, 28
    connectedness, 29, 95
    relationship, 5, 29, 35, 51, 52
"identifying the between" [Buber], 48,
        51
"imagining the real" [Buber], 3, 21,
        44
inclusion, 76
    act of [Buber], 3, 12, 21, 22, 44, 45,
        48, 50, 51, 72, 88
    concept of, 41
individualism:
    vs. attachment, 5–15
    vs. collectivity, 20
Inger, I. B., 1, 18, 20, 22, 43, 44, 45, 47
Inger, J., 1, 18, 20, 43, 44, 45, 47

intuition, internal experience of,
    legitimization of, 34
irreverence, 41
    vs. reverence, 42

Jackson, D., 44
Jung, C. G., 6

Keeney, B., 38
knowing, nature of, 41

Lane, G., 41
language, as power issue, 40
"Learning III" phenomenon [Bateson],
    44
Luckman, T., 31

Mahler, M., 6
Maturana, H. R., 37
meanings, constructions of, 47
Menninger, K. A., 12
Milan team, 34
mothers:
    and daughters, relationship
        between, 8
    and sons, relationship between, 7

naming, reliance on, 15

objectivity, 3, 11–12, 13, 15, 21, 22, 23,
    25, 27, 37, 38, 39, 44
    as oppressor of science, 39
    reliance on, 15
    vs. subjectivity, 38
observer, 37, 38
    and observed, 37, 38

Papp, P., 7
passive–aggressive personality, 14
Penn, P., 37
personality:
    borderline, 14
    passive–aggressive, 14
persuasion, as power issue, 40
Plato, 38
Polyani, M., 38
power:
    inherent in all relationships, 39

    use of by therapists, 39
Prata, G., 34
process of therapy, vs. content of
    therapy, 37
psychotherapy, ethical perspective
    for, 2

Ray, W., 41
reflecting team, 32–35
reflectivity, in thinking, 40
reframing, positive, 91

Sampson, E. E., 8, 9
Segal, L., 37
self:
    -healing tautology, 19
    and internal psychological
        changes, 19
Selvini-Palazzoli, M., 34, 44
separation, 8, 10, 38, 52, 113
    vs. attachment, 6
    of male child, 7
    of child:
        from father, 8
        from mother, 7–9
    impact of, on mother, 8
Shabatay, V., 45
shadow clients, 10
Shaffer, P., 24
Silverstein, O., 7, 8
simulation, of family interview, 66
Skorpen, A., 32
social construction therapy, 115
social control, recourse to, as power
    issue, 40
sociopathic character, 14
subjectivity, 24, 37, 38
Sullivan, H. S., 6
symmetry, 86, 111
    vs. complementarity, 75, 115

tautology, self-healing, 19
team, reflecting, 32–35
therapist, hierarchical position of, 33
therapy:
    ethically based [Buber], 44–52
    process vs. content, 37
thinking, categorical, 24

time, perceptions of, 19
"turning towards the other", vs.
    "bending back to oneself"
        [Buber], 49

uncertainty:
    crises of, 3
    tolerating, 48

Von Foerster, H., 37
Von Glasersfeld, E., 37

Walters, M., 7, 8
Watzlawick, P., 37, 44
Weakland, J., 44
White, M., 44
Winnicott, D. W., 6